THE GOLDEN YEARS

Match Fishing Memories

Billy Makin

KBO Authors

Copyright © 2021 Billy Makin

All rights reserved.

No part of this book may be reproduced, or stored in a retrieval system, or transmitted in any form or by any means, electronic, mechanical, photocopying, recording, or otherwise, without express written permission of the publisher except for the use of brief quotations in a book review.

Enquiries: admin@kboauthors.com
Cover design: Liam Dale 2021

CONTENTS

Title Page
Copyright
THE GOLDEN YEARS   1
INTRODUCTION   2
Chapter 1   4
Chapter 2   9
Chapter 3   21
Chapter 4   31
Chapter 5   40
Chapter 6   50
Chapter 7   65
Chapter 8   75
Chapter 9   83
Chapter 10   100
Chapter 11   108
Chapter 12   119
Chapter 13   130
Chapter 14   135
Chapter 15   144
Chapter 16   152
Chapter17   162

Chapter 18	171
Chapter 19	184
Chapter 20	196
Chapter 21	207
Chapter 22	218
Chapter 23	228
Chapter 24	241
Chapter 25	260
Chapter 26	269
Chapter 27	274
Chapter 28	280
Chapter 29	297
Chapter 30	310
Chapter 31	317
Chapter 32	326
Chapter 33	336
Would you please consider leaving a review?	343
Books by Billy Makin	344
THE AUTHOR	346

THE GOLDEN YEARS

Match Fishing Memories

WHEN REAL ANGLERS ROAMED THE PLANET

DEDICATED TO FRIENDS LONG GONE AND THOSE THAT ARE STILL TREADING WATER.

WE ARE PART OF A BROTHERHOOD – A UNIVERSAL BONDING THAT NEITHER TIME NOR LANGUAGE CAN PART.

WE ARE FISHERMEN.

INTRODUCTION

The book is very much a compilation of the monthly articles that I have written for Matchfishing Magazine, coupled with occasional anecdotes from my Facebook pages.

Few people have ever written about the good old days of matchfishing, with barely a mention in the angling press of the people responsible for the myriad of minor tackle innovations and inventions, which when brought together contribute immensely to the modern-day match angler's armoury.

Without match fishermen, progress would have been considerably slower as competition accelerates innovation, whereas a laissez faire approach is a recipe for stagnation.

The only real constant in the world of match fishing has always been the fish.

Fish have never really moved on from the time when our ancestors targeted them for food to their present-day temporary confinement in the match angler's keepnet.

They can be finicky to the point of exasperation, whilst for no apparent reason, will inexplicably develop an uncontrollable desire to relocate to an angler's keepnet.

Understanding fish is an insoluble yet intriguing exercise that generations of match anglers have puzzled over when looking for that slight mystical edge over the competition.

I don't think that there is a magic bullet that guarantees success.

There is a god given gift which when coupled with hard work and dedication elevates the good anglers to the status of legends.

I have fished with and against these legends.

I was privileged.

>   I AM FROM THE GOLDEN AGE OF MATCHFISHING.

◆ ◆ ◆

CHAPTER 1

WE WERE BORN TO FISH

Every story must have a beginning.

I suppose that the story of fishing goes back to man's first sight of water, be it a river, lake, or sea, and once he discovered that beneath the surface of the water lay food, he became interested and has spent the last two hundred thousand years working out ways of extracting that food in order to eat it.

From the time that our ancestors first climbed down from the jungle canopy, millions of years of genetic programming have inevitably led to an instinct that not only helped to keep them alive but also fulfilled an irresistible urge to hunt and fish that has never gone away.

Perhaps this is how match-fishing first began; the sublime coming together of both evolved instinct and the need to prove male dominance.

I know that many female types go fishing, but generally speaking, it is a male-dominated sport, and the mere sight of maggots and worms tends to send women into fits of apoplexy.

The female of the species did not evolve to hunt, that was the male's job, and regardless of modern-day feminist's views on equality, even remote jungle tribeswomen still follow ancient role-play traditions without the need to burn their bras or to emasculate their men by insisting on a vegan-only diet.

In our present world we no longer need to fish to eat, yet deep down, possibly millions of years long past, we developed a hunting instinct that cannot be displaced by simple moralistic sentiment.

Men were born to fish – get used to it.

If we don't eat them, so what?

We don't eat golf balls, yet some men spend half their lives trying to beat the living daylights out of a piece of plastic.

Men like to compete against each other – always have done – always will do.

This competitive spirit combined with an inbred hunting instinct created the modern-day match fisherman.

It created me.

Even God makes the occasional blunder.

* * * * *

My match fishing career began in the time-honoured fashion of Club Fishing, my first-ever big match success coming at the age of 13.

During my teenage years, I became known as "The Boy with the Golden Arm" thanks to a rather silly article in the local press after catching a "monster" bream from Carr Mill Dam, a water not thought to contain bream, and the name jokingly stuck, being inextricably linked to my ability to draw every known flyer at the Dam.

THE ARCHES AT CARR MILL DAM

This uncanny ability to draw known fish-holding swims never really left me and various people that I travelled with over the years often shook their heads in disbelief as flyer after flyer seemingly stuck to my fingers at the drawbag.

After university and a brief spell in the army, I moved to the Midlands from my native North West and had to reinvent myself as a completely different all-round type of angler.

My commercially produced floats, particularly the popular Canal Greys, became an important item in most match angler's tackle boxes.

After selling my float manufacturing business I moved on to build Makin Fisheries, the first commercial fishery of its kind in Britain consisting of 18 lakes and over 500 swims.

I now live in Thailand with my Thai wife and own a couple of bars for ex-pats and holiday makers.

From my early days in the Midlands during the late seventies I often wrote for David Hall's magazines, but on selling my lakes to British Waterways at the turn of the millennium, I left the country and resolved to retire and do sweet Fanny Adams for the rest of my life with as much style as possible.

For some inexplicable reason I became an author; I enjoy writing books, and a fertile, some would say perverse sense of humour coupled with an over-active imagination has helped me along.

One morning, quite out of the blue, I received an email from the editor of Matchfishing Magazine asking me if I would like to do a series of articles for him.

'Why not?' I thought.

You will find lots of name dropping and why shouldn't there be?

Over the years, I have fished with and against some of the finest anglers of their, or indeed, any generation.

I have beaten them, and I have been thrashed by them – all that is irrelevant.

I was proud to know them, I respected them, and in many cases, as a kid, I idolised them.

Oh, by the way, after a thirty-year break from match fishing, I am back in the saddle here in Thailand and loving every minute of it. It may be different to my matchfishing days in England, but the common factors of great company, camaraderie, and fish make it no less enjoyable.

CHAPTER 2

A CHAP CALLED HARRY

It is now four am in the morning and I cannot sleep.

Something is wrong.

Sleep has rarely been a problem for me. Normally, I leave my bar in Pattaya, Thailand in the early hours, arriving back in the apartment around 2 am, and after a shower I am asleep before my head hits the pillow.

Today, I am in a small Thai jungle village for a few days of torture with Rinda, my Thai wife, and lying here in bed I am now enveloped by an overwhelming cacophony of silence.

That is the problem - it is too quiet.

The silence is so loud that it is deafening, the slightest sound being amplified a thousand times.

The mice are wearing clogs.

I need to hear the sounds of the city that never sleeps; no, not New York, Pattaya, my adopted hometown; Pattaya is far noisier than the big apple; music, motorbikes and laughter ring out throughout the night and into the early hours of the morning, all of which seems to have a therapeutic way of relaxing the mind by neutralizing and cancelling each other out.

My mind begins to wander.

I feel myself moving back in time.

Back to a time before time itself began.

* * * * *

Dad is going fishing and I am not going with him.

I burst into tears.

"For God's sake take him with you Bill," thankfully mum has taken sides. "He will be under my feet and sulk all day if you don't take him."

That was the day that both my obsession and my journey began - the day that defined my life and was to lead me around much of the world, not just in the pursuit of fish, but also into a life-changing dream of almost magical reality - a dream that was to become a profession - a dream-like obsession that enabled me to earn a living for doing what I would have willingly done for free.

WHEN I HAD HAIR – DAD ON THE RIGHT WITH THE SHIELD

Daniel, the Matchfishing Magazine editor at the time, had asked me to do a series on the history of match fishing based very much on the postings that I do on a regular basis on my Facebook page. To do this, the series had to be very much autobiographical, taking in not just my own experiences gathered during my match fishing life, but also those of the people that I have met and fished with over the period that is often described as the Golden Age of Match Fishing.

Household names of match fishing heroes flashed before my eyes; friends, acquaintances, and rivals all roll off the tongue - a roll call of names that in their own way all contributed to their place in angling history and tackle development; men who designed floats, swing tips, bread punches - men who discovered and perfected caster fishing, waggler fishing, all types of freshwater fishing.

Match anglers were constantly on the lookout for the slightest improvement that would give them an edge over the field - money was much harder to come by then.

These men did not go into a tackle shop to buy their tackle.

Little more than a cane rod, a centrepin reel, and the basic hook line and sinker existed when I was a kid. Everything had to be designed and made at home.

When dad was a young man, throwing any kind of bread-based groundbait into a canal was unthinkable - food was much too valuable to feed to the fish.

The world had barely moved on from the 2nd world war, and many coarse fish often found their way onto the family table alongside the occasional rabbit; this before myxomatosis exacted its murderous plague-like ravages on what had become a staple diet for many a poor family.

Groundbait consisted of finely riddled soil and hook bait was chopped worms or homebred maggots. Occasionally, a couple of slices of bread would be smuggled out of the kitchen, but the array of modern baits was not even a dream on a distant horizon.

* * * * *

I was a lucky kid I suppose, often too smart for my own good as I was often told, yet I was always willing to learn and absorb every morsel of information relating to what was to become quite an over-riding obsession. Many were the nights that I would lie awake for hours, my body in a cold bed in an unheated room, my mind wandering the banks of the local canal, pondering how to explain and navigate the problems that the previous week's fishing had thrown up, problems that in years to come would only be solved by tackle and tactics that hadn't yet been invented.

Unlike most of my contemporaries, I had never needed to undergo the long-established, yet almost obligatory bent pin and worm fishing apprenticeship. Dad was a pretty good angler, and each generation of cast-off tackle was passed down to me together with the knowledge and experience that accompanied it.

* * * * *

My match fishing story begins with a Bolton club called the Kings Head.

I would be around 12 at the time, and as only wealthy people had cars in those days, thousands of coaches left the industrial Northern cities of Lancashire and Yorkshire early every Sunday morning in search of grass, fresh air, sunlight, and water.

Specially laid on steam trains travelled to distant horizons loaded with expectant anglers, all glad to be experiencing a day of freedom once again from the near servitude that pervaded and strangled their weekday soul and physical being.

Grim-faced coal miners, factory workers, and steel men saw little daylight during these back-breaking weekdays, and the fresh air of the countryside allowed them to clear their minds and lungs of the grime and coal dust.

For the Kings Head anglers, the Lancaster canal was almost always the venue of choice, and mid-day invariably found me sat by the canal bridge riding shotgun over the 30 sets of the angler's already assembled tackle as they indulged in the mandatory lunchtime drinking session, the bonding interlude that split the morning match from the afternoon match.

All the tackle was left set up from the morning match, and on leaving the pub, they would make the draw for the afternoon match and were immediately ready for action.

My reward was a free match as a thank you for looking after this tackle.

Now at the time, a chap called Harry Settle was the king pin, winning match after match - not big weights by today's standards, with somewhere around 2lb usually being enough to secure first prize.

Being the inquisitive, devious little blighter that I was, I seized the opportunity to check out Harry's set up as he was drinking with the rest of the anglers; this I then followed up by opening his wicker tackle box and examining the contents, one eye always directed in the direction of the pub as an insurance policy.

What were those curious pieces of metal with holes in the end I wondered, and why did a couple of them have a piece of bread stuck in them?

There was also a slice of bread that was full of holes.

Harry had easily won the morning match, so could this be the key to his success?

Harry was too smart to throw his bread away and reveal the secret of this success, and he certainly never thought that a kid would have the cheeky audacity to go through his tackle box.

He didn't reckon on someone like me being around - big mistake.

One of his bread punches, as they later became known, and one of his floats stuck to my fingers like glue - I couldn't shake them off no matter how hard I tried.

As the slightly inebriated anglers left the pub and noisily made their way to the canal, we all made the draw, and what was to become known as "The Golden Arm" at the draw bag appeared for the first time, and out popped the end peg, right on the point of the wides.

And so it came to pass that I was to witness the sweet, intoxicating, almost addictive scent, and taste of match fishing success for the first time that afternoon.

I was instantly hooked, and like any addict, the pursuit of my next fix took precedence over all other forms of life's pleasures that growing up had to offer.

Harry Settle had to settle for second place that afternoon, and viewed my 3lb of roach suspiciously, while I in turn prayed that he wouldn't notice the missing float and bread punch, nor the slice of bread that I had taken to keep them company.

Bursting with pride, I just had to tell dad everything that evening and received the not unexpected slap round the head as a reward.

Scrumping apples was acceptable if they appeared on the family table - stealing someone else's property wasn't and never would be.

I may have been brought up in a poor mining village but maintaining standards was cast in stone and essential to everyday life – standards were never compromised.

How times have changed.

He did however relent somewhat when I presented him with a pretty good copy of both the float and the bread punch a couple of days later, and unlike Harry, we managed to keep the mysteries of the bread punch secret for several years.

On dad's strict instructions, I returned Harry's float and bread punch the following Sunday during the mid-day Lancaster canal beer sojourn, and my indiscretion was soon forgotten.

The cat was now out of the bag, but only for dad and me.

MODERN DAY BREAD PUNCHES

Everything has to start somewhere, and like every angling invention, sooner or later the discovery leaks out and eventually finds its way into the tackle shop, and so it is with every item of tackle that the modern-day matchman now takes for granted.

Interestingly, without being aware of it at the time, Harry's balsa float pretty much provided the blueprint for the canal grey float that I began to manufacture in my Hinckley float factory some years later, a float that broke the mould and literally sold in the millions.

I have always gratefully accepted the credit and accolades that came with the popularity of the float, but in all honesty, it was little more than a copy, sneakily misappropriated from its true designer a little over 15 years earlier.

* * * * *

I have mentally, temporarily returned to the Thai jungle village, and sleep is now out of the question as the dawn chorus of countless cockerels has begun. To begin with there was one solitary bird, then another one, soon to be followed by a whole orchestral cock a doodle symphony, accompanied by the village dogs - a solid impenetrable wall of sound that not even the dead can sleep through.

The sun swiftly awakens the jungle village, and the coming daylight once again takes me willingly and magically back in time.

I move on from the Kings Head trips and begin to subconsciously taste the excitement of what for me would become the Holy Grail of my life - match fishing.

My inquisitive young mind once again bursts into life and puts in a welcome appearance; vague images begin to take shape as the gift of almost total recall invades my senses and magically moves me back in time.

*****

Dad is alive again; he is still a relatively young man and is standing in front of me at the draw.

The place looks familiar.

The ghosts of men long reduced to ashes surround me as they discuss the day's prospects.

Tears of nostalgia appear as deja vu turns daydream into assumed reality.

I am at a place called Saltiforth on the Leeds/Liverpool canal, somewhere pretty close to Yorkshire bandit country, and in five days I will enter the beginning of my second year as a teenager.

This is to be my first experience of a real match and I feel nervous as the Golden Arm enters the draw bag.

"Nice draw Billy, but not quite good enough - you are two pegs away from me and you know what that means."

Harry Settle is looking over my shoulder and is introducing my inexperienced youthful naivety to my first glimpse of mind games.

Is he becoming worried about me I wonder?

Is he deliberately trying to undermine my confidence?

I had already beaten him on a couple of occasions the previous season on the King Head trips, yet Harry still held the whip hand during most of the matches.

Each passing week saw me slowly close the gap, but deep down I knew that I wasn't yet ready for Harry Settle.

No one on the Northern match circuit was.

Harry Settle was the undisputed "King of the Cut".

"One day Harry," I whispered under my breath. "One day soon my time will come."

CHAPTER 3

SHOWDOWN

I had tested Harry's mettle on numerous occasions in my first year of club fishing, and other than a couple of times, I had always come out second best.

Harry had become a force to be reckoned with on the then limited OPEN match scene, and when not so employed, always travelled with the Kings Head coach.

Slowly, inch by inch, and ounce by ounce, I was progressing and improving. Harry could sense that I was closing the gap on him, yet I was still some way from beating him in a head-to-head encounter.

I had an ally though – a very special ally.

Every week, dad and I travelled to Benny Ashurst's house to collect our bait for the coming weekend, and although Benny and dad were long time deadly rivals, for some strange reason, Benny treated me almost like a son and held nothing back when dispensing advice.

I questioned everything and forgot nothing.

What an unbelievable bonus this was for a wide-eyed kid who lived and dreamed match fishing and nothing else. Girls were of a different species altogether and were to remain so until my late teens, and even then, only during the 3-month closed season when not whipping hooks or making floats.

A CLASSIC FROM BEFORE TIME ITSELF BEGAN

Benny, along with Coventry's Billy Lane, was one of the two best anglers in the country, if not the world, and were to remain so until a semi-Bohemian gypsy type, name of Ivan Marks came along. In later years, Ivan himself was to become a mentor.

Many a Friday evening was spent in Benny's company and my infinitely limitless sponge like brain for all things fishing absorbed every morsel on offer.

"Think of sparrows in thi back yard young un," Benny had said. "Once thi gets first un theer, t'others will follow. Don't scare off first un, tek thi time, never rush things, and build up thi swim slowly."

"And another thing young un," he went on. "Don't think that

because thi can't see any fish, thi can't see thee. Sit well back from th'edge of cut, and don't let anybody stand behind thi."

These words of advice were to remain with me throughout my match fishing days, and on this particular day, maybe, just maybe, they would provide the edge in beating the tour de force that was Harry Settle.

* * * * *

I have again returned to my deja vu, almost reality induced fantasy world and I am surrounded by familiar ghosts of the past - ghosts so real that I can almost reach out and touch them.

The date is now October the 13th, 1963, and I have tears of joy running down my face and I am once again in the pub at Saltiforth on the Leeds Liverpool canal, and in my hands is the most beautiful thing on earth.

I will be fourteen in five days, and unknown to me, dad has been saving for my birthday present.

I am speechless and open-mouthed as I open my eyes to the best birthday present anyone in the world has ever received.

No one on earth is strong enough or can run fast enough to wrest away from me my new 12-foot Tonkin and Greenheart match rod, built and created by Frank Constantine, a master rod builder from Bolton.

Its mesmerising dream-like whipping securing the tiny wire rings and underneath the gleaming varnish is my name - "Billy

Makin Junior."

THE GREATEST BIRTHDAY PRESENT EVER

Tears flood my eyes and I almost have to walk away.

Harry Settle smiles and throws a knowing wink, at the same time slowly shaking his head to one side - almost a superior wink if such a thing exists.

This is a challenge, a blatant challenge for all to see - darn it - I wink back and meet his eyes full on, nodding slowly and purposefully, a faint smile temporarily appearing.

I visually accept the challenge, mentally picturing the Shakespearean lesson in school that very week. 'Lay on, Macduff, and damn'd be him that first cries, 'Hold, enough.'

Harry's eyes open wide with surprise.

I have only been drafted into the team at the last minute as one of Dad's Kings Head team has missed the coach, so instead of fishing alongside the bridge during the match, I now have to make up the numbers in the 250 peg Winter League match.

It's funny really how I can have total recall of one single day in my life so long ago when I can't even remember what I had for breakfast this morning.

Delving deep into long forgotten and unused memory banks, I now have to close my eyes and try to isolate this one particular fishing memory from a million others, all filed away in some dusty storage compartment deep within my brain.

I mentioned how I had acquired this new-fangled bread punch thing from Harry Settle's tackle box during the obligatory alcoholic break between the Kings Head morning and afternoon matches, and so, together with Dad, the pair of us, plus Harry, were the only ones in the match equipped with this new technological marvel.

I had also relieved Harry's tackle box of one of his bread punch floats, and for the past few weeks had been working on ways of improving them. Being a "sickly" child when the time and occasion suited, I had spent quite a few days down the local canal both "recuperating" and working on different ways of fishing and feeding with this new wonder bait, becoming quite proficient and increasingly successful on the Kings Head coach trips, and was by now fishing both the morning and afternoon matches.

At the age of 13, the memory banks are still quite empty, and being pretty much an obsessive, I had resolved to fill them with as much fishing information as possible, almost certainly at the expense of the boring maths, physics and chemistry being taught at Leigh Grammar school.

I was only ever present in body, my mind rarely leaving the canal towpath.

As far as I was aware, Newton, Pythagoras, and Archimedes never went fishing so were of little interest to me.

* * * * *

My swim was only about 100 yards from the pub on a bend where the canal widened out a little, and 2 pegs away was Harry Settle.

I hid both my float and bread punch when Harry came and stood behind me for a chat shortly before the starting whistle.

Benny Ashurst's words flashed before my eyes. "Don't let anybody stand behind thi young un." He had said.

I recognized Harry's game as he stood right at the water's edge of my swim.

I stood up, and still talking to Harry, walked towards his peg, standing as close to the edge as possible, and determined to remain there for several minutes until the starting whistle sounded.

This had obviously been Harry's initial ploy, but I had turned the tables on him and now he couldn't really say too much.

I was slowly beginning to grow up a little - not yet streetwise but learning.

The whistle went, and I quietly walked back to my swim, positioning my wicker basket a good yard back from the water, and, caressing the most beautiful thing on earth, perfectly balanced by an Alcocks Ariel centrepin reel, I swung out my modified version of Harry's float, below which was a tiny piece of bread from my replica of Harry's bread punch.

THE FAMOUS ALLCOCKS AERIAL CENTREPIN

The float disappeared on the drop, and a couple of minutes later, a beautiful fit brown trout found its way into my keepnet.

The next 4 casts produced 4 more trout before I finally caught a roach.

We later discovered that the waterboard had stocked a couple of thousand of the blighters that week and everyone in the match was plagued by them.

As the match went on, I began to catch more roach and less trout, until after what seemed like little more than a couple of hours, 5 hours had passed, and the whistle sounded for the end of the match.

I had enjoyed myself but still felt a little deflated.

Harry had spent the entire match with his rod in one hand and his landing net in the other - I had been slaughtered.

I had foolishly accepted Harry Settle's visual challenge in the pub.

I was not yet ready to compete on equal terms with the "King of the Cut".

"Tha can't weigh them theer trout son", the scales man said, so we spent the next 5 minutes reducing a near double figure net of fish to 4 pounds 4 ounces and 4 drams.

Harry Settle was amazed to find himself in second place that day with a couple of ounces less. The dozens of fish that I had painfully watched him net had been trout, in many cases the same one that he had returned 5 minutes earlier.

Beating the best canal angler in the North West felt good.

My birthday present felt better.

My match fishing addiction was now full-blown and all-consuming.

* * * * *

On reflection, over 50 years later, putting the trout in my keepnet that day was almost certainly the advantage (quite illegal but not intentionally so) that turned the tables on Harry.

Trout can be pretty stupid creatures, and once I had stuffed every single one from my swim into my keepnet I could concentrate on the roach. Harry returned them and continued to catch the same dozen trout repeatedly.

Cunning stunt really.

I now had enough money to buy one of them new-fangled casting reels that Benny had told me about.

"Tha needs one o them if tha wants to catch caster fish," he had said.

I couldn't wait for Friday afternoon.

I just had to tell Benny about my win and to ask him about this caster fishing.

There were many empty drawers in my memory bank that needed filling.

I was soon to enter the guarded and virtually exclusive memory bank of the great man himself - Benny Ashurst.

I bet Harry Settle knew bugger all about caster fishing and I wasn't about to tell him.

CHAPTER 4

EVEN YOUNGER

Although my match fishing career began in the grim hinterland known as the North West, I gradually expanded my fishing horizons to include the Midlands following a brief spell in the army.

I now however find myself moving even farther back in time - you will see why this is important, not only from a fishing perspective but also because of a long-lost social landscape that in our clinically clean, sanitized, 21st-century environment appears to be almost medieval.

Around this time, shortly after Adam tempted Eve into eating an apple and talked her into removing the fig leaf placed to keep the flies away, I emerged from a perfectly formed embryo into a boy often described by neighbours as the living reincarnation of Satan himself. I attended St Anne's junior school, a little more than a hundred yards from my home, where I continued to wreak havoc on any of Gods' less fortunate creations that chose to wear skirts.

Next to the junior school was a slaughterhouse, where an endless procession of animals volunteered their services to the butchery trade, and around the same time each morning, dozens of pigs began their terrified squealing having figured out their fate from the all-pervading smell of blood and death before being turned into bacon butties and pork chops.

Alongside the slaughterhouse, separated by no more than a few yards of wasteland were Simeon Johnsons' piggery, one of only two places in Britain that bred squatts, the other one being Pascals, a few miles away on the outskirts of Leigh.

SQUATTS

I did mention the word medieval, and in our sanitized society it is difficult to imagine a junior school next to both a slaughterhouse and a piggery come maggot breeding establishment, whose smells and sounds have never left me to this day.

Every Wednesday I watched a dozen or so large biscuit tins of squatts being loaded onto the piggery van on their way to Tyldesley rail station, each one bearing the address W H Lane Fishing Tackle - Coventry; that's right, the one and only Billy Lane, a name that was to become embedded deep in my psyche as I progressed towards my teenage years.

Now Alan Johnson, the grandson of Simeon, and I were friends and sat together at school. As I became more and more interested in fishing, I developed what some may call a morbid fascination at the link between the slaughterhouse and the piggery/maggot farm.

Why didn't Simeon Johnson feed his squatts on meat?

I found out exactly what they ate, as one evening, Alan took me into the piggery when all was quiet and showed me the closely guarded secret process.

COMMERCIAL SQUATT FARM

I already knew that rotting meat grew maggots, and many were the times that the neighbours complained to mum about the smells that occasionally wafted from our back yard shed, as being a deft hand with an air gun I kept the local feral pigeon and rabbit population under control.

I became a closet maggot breeder, quite an obsessive, and spent much of my growing up years experimenting with different maggots, feeding materials, and dyes.

As trouble seemed to be my middle name, (Lucifer being a constant companion), during my teenage year's dad found me a job at Pendlebury's, a Leigh maggot farm, where I eagerly learned the processes involved in breeding them commercially.

I have detailed my exploits at the maggot farm in my book Fishing and Testicles, suffice to say, when breeding hundreds of gallons of maggots weekly, the trouble I got into was magnified many times over.

As unlikely as it seems nowadays when every item of tackle can be found packaged and labelled together with instructions in the local tackle shop, there were no spade end hooks when I was growing up, and the smallest hook available was a size 20's. This was fine for a caster or a maggot, but a single squatt on a thick gauge wire size 20's hook that was tied onto the line with silk, together with a glob of glue, looked and was out of place.

One particular day as I was sat on the Lancaster canal guarding the club angler's tackle during the mid-day beer break, I had a little dabble by the canal bridge; bites were hard to come by, and I was so convinced that the hook was the problem that I snipped it off and tied the squatt onto the line.

Every cast produced a bite almost immediately, most of them as the bait fell through the water.

The hook was most definitely the problem - it was too big and too heavy, being of pretty thick gauge wire by today's standards.

I became fascinated with the problem, often lying awake for half the night trying to think of a solution, and then one day as I watched mum knitting, I had my eureka moment. Dad was intrigued as I explained the idea to him, and the next evening he arrived home from work at the local mine with a small set of pliers.

I had managed to obtain a box of very fine wire hooks from the local tackle shop, and by bending them around one of mum's thinner knitting needles, I could reduce the gape quite considerably before they snapped. A good third of the shank was then snipped off which left a flattened section at the end.

Not only had I created a passable spade end hook, I also had a barbless hook, as the barb had been flattened during the bending process.

By bending the hook around an even thinner darning needle, I could now go down to a barbless, spade end sized 24's by today's standards.

Are you beginning to understand now how life was at the time?

We had to think.

We had to improvise.

We had to invent the wheel.

Imagine a world without mobile phones - someone had to invent them and so it was with fishing tackle.

If you weren't happy with your tackle, you either redesigned it to your own specifications or you became an also-ran in match fishing terms.

The nearest to a true innovator that I have come across in more modern times has been Andy Findlay. The Fin completely redesigned the method feeder, and for several years seemed to have the commercial carp fishing game as a second income.

I was now ready to supplement my bread punch techniques with the proper hook for squatt fishing.

It was around this time that the importance of the slaughterhouse came into play.

One day, Alan brought to my home a tin of half-grown squatts that he had smuggled out of the piggery.

My mind went into overdrive; how could I turn these half-grown squatts into monsters for the hook?

Believe it or not, either by luck or divine inspiration, I got it right pretty much the first time without too much experimenting.

A couple of slices of bread soaked in blood from the slaughterhouse, together with the cream off the top of the milk bottle produced absolute pythons, and I now had probably the best canal bait in the country - squatts so big, fat, and juicy that they could barely move.

Coupled with my barbless size 24's hooks, monster squatts, Harry Settle's floats and bread punches, AND a fair chunk of Benny Ashurst's angling knowledge and coaching, I have to say that few people on the canal banking was better equipped, and what I lacked in experience, I more than made up for in dare I say, "State of the Art Technology", because that is really what it was at the time.

In modern times, the art of breeding pedigree maggots has been confined to the scrapbook of history, nevertheless, with the resurgence of silverfish matches, maybe - just maybe - a little knowledge can go a long way and deliver the edge that all match anglers are looking for.

Now accompanying the squatts on the canal bank was a maggot that in Lancashire terms is known as a "Special". This is a completely different animal from anything that most anglers have ever seen.

It resembles a giant fat squatt, has 2 little black "eyes", and unlike all other maggots, always crawls backwards.

The best medium for breeding these specials is bran, sprinkled with a bit of pee and a good dollop of full cream milk. If I wanted monsters, blood from the slaughterhouse was added once the maggots were half-grown, and if you wanted the best bait that angling has ever come up with, the blood and milk were mixed with annatto, producing a buttery yellow bait that skimmers would fight over, and fellow anglers would die for.

As I entered my teenage years, the angling press began to become very excited over a new wonder bait that was becoming popular on the Midlands' bream circuit, the gozzer.

Around the time that Benny Ashurst was becoming famous for his caster exploits, so too was Billy Lane, helped along with some tremendous bream catches because of his gozzer fishing.

Billy's recipe for breeding gozzers was quite simple and involved no more than opening up a dead pigeon, placing it in a dark shady place, and when "blown", wrapping it in newspaper and dropping it into a container of bran - nature doing the rest.

Was the gozzer a new wonder bait?

It was better than a commercial maggot for bream, that's for sure, but in all honesty, it could never really compete with a fat, juicy, annatto special - honest, but us Northerners weren't going to let the Midlanders know this.

Interestingly, if pinkies were the intended bait, the pigeon, or better still a sheep or pig's heart, was left covered for a couple of days until its aroma became noticeable. The gozzer fly would only "blow" fresh meat, and as soon as the smell arrived, so did the greenbottle fly, the parent of the pinkie.

Again, the application of annatto to the half-grown pinkie helped to produce a bait good enough to eat, and a further alternative bait was now available that took some beating for roach.

Now all this may seem a little unnecessary in modern-day terms, but you need to put things into a time scale perspective. Matches on the Northern canal circuit were decided by ounces, not pounds; five hundred entry matches rarely needed more than 3 or 4 pounds to win, often being in the 2 to 3 lb range, and a selection of different, yet top quality baits was often the deciding factor when the money was paid out. Money was extremely hard to come by in those days, and with a bookmaker being present at most matches, the competition was fierce.

Fish seemed to be much more choosey over their meals in my early match fishing career, and a pedigree bait change often resulted in a fished-out swim producing that all-important extra bite or two.

I guess that nothing has changed that much over the years.

Even carp, the spawn of Satan, seem to change their preferences during the course of a match, and having observed the best anglers that the country has produced in this field over the years, the man who recognizes this mid-match change in preference invariably gives himself an edge over his competitors.

And so my life moved on.

I was fortunate enough to have avoided the bent pin, cotton, and worms of my contemporaries, helped along by an obsessive curiosity and invaluable guidance from both dad and Benny Ashurst.

CHAPTER 5

FLOATS AND SUCH

I was sat in my Thai bar one evening gently sipping a Tiger beer and just watching the world and the working girls go by. I was pretty much in a vacant rather than a pensive mood; it had been a quiet evening and I was tired.

My mind began to move back in time as I wondered if, at this advanced stage of maturity (early middle age; I refuse to move on beyond this point), I would still be foolhardy enough to venture forth and face the winter elements on the Oxford canal at one of Pat O'Connor's wonderful matches.

I closed my eyes and drifted into the twilight zone where memories turned to clear reality as my Canal Grey float disappeared beneath the icy cold surface that was a hole in the ice, and one of God's finest creations came to hand.

It was cold to the touch - I could definitely feel it as it wriggled in my hand.

This was no longer a daydream, this was real, the fish was alive and so was I, the single bloodworm hanging from its' lips was also alive.

I was no longer in Thailand - I was home - the canal was my home - if there is a God, this is why he created me.

I was born to fish.

I felt a pang of guilt as I slipped the exquisite gudgeon into my keepnet without even allowing it to finish its' meal, still, he would soon be meeting a few of his mates as bites were now beginning to come thick and fast.

I momentarily opened my eyes as a ladyboy walked by holding hands with a grossly overweight 60 something-year-old chap - my gudgeon catching momentum was broken, I had returned to the present – darn it.

I studied the ladyboy trying to understand the attraction.

He was beautiful; an aquiline face, long perfect legs with the tiniest mini skirt, tight bottom, slim waist, and perfectly formed silicon breasts striving to escape from of a low-cut top - a sculptured man-made model woman with a body that most Western women could only ever dream of.

I like it here in Thailand, but at that one moment in time I wanted to return home, I wanted to return to my Oxford canal home, I wanted to return to a swim full of gudgeon so desperately that it hurt.

I closed my eyes and continued my journey back in time.

I was moving quickly, much too quickly and missed my stop. There are times when my mental time machine runs away with itself and settles wherever it wants to regardless of my intentions.

I found myself a little more than 8 years old, and as usual, I was causing as much mischief as possible down the local lake or lodge as we knew it. My gang and I were catching newts on pieces of worm. There were no hooks, the newts simply refused to let go of the worm once their jaws locked on.

The tackle was simple enough and consisted of a whippy branch broken from one of the weeping willow trees that lined the banking of the old lake, a length of cotton, and a matchstick for a float. A loop was tied in the cotton and the worm slipped into the noose.

Bites were signalled by the matchstick being held a couple of inches below the surface as the newt got to grips with a worm that was often twice its' size.

I did have access to much better tackle than this in the form of dad's cast-offs, but this was much more fun.

Often, a fish, almost always a perch, would grab the worm and try to shake it free. We never managed to get one to hold on long enough for us to get hold of but occasionally we did get them to clear the water before they released the worm, then they invariably waited around for a second go so we had to move around in search of perch free newt fishing.

The rules stated newts only.

This was match fishing at its' most intense, each newt being dropped into a water-filled jam jar, with bragging rights carried forward for several days for the victor.

Mum saw me at mealtimes only. I was a stranger in my own home and the thought of spending one single second of daylight in the house was unimaginable.

* * * * *

As a kid there were only 2 types of float available in the tackle shops, one being the infamous Perch Bobber and the other one the ubiquitous porcupine quill.

PERCH BOBBERS

The porcupine quill was a weapon in waiting, and no matter how carefully you handled it, one or other of the ends always embedded itself in either your hand or finger. The Perch Bobber was a little more benign and consisted of a brightly painted lump of cork with some form of cane running through the middle. It was so named because its' extreme buoyancy prevented anything short of a blue whale pulling it under - it just bobbed around creating a series of rings on the surface whenever you had a bite, plus of course the only fish we kids were ever likely to catch was the ever-obliging perch.

Neither of the two options was satisfactory, and so all matchmen made their own floats using a variety of materials and designs, the favourite among the Northern canal anglers being the humble crow quill.

I well remember arriving home in triumph one day carrying a dead crow with my air gun pellet still embedded in its' head - I had sat under the tree for hours waiting for it to return.

* * * * *

Around this time, Angling Times ran a competition to find the country's best float maker, the competition being won by a young chap called Peter Drennon, Peter capitalizing on his success and becoming one of the world's leading fishing tackle manufacturers.

Over the years, joining Peter in the ranks of commercial float makers came Middy, Ultra, Continental pole, Gerry Woodcock, and Ray Nimmo.

* * * * *

I guess that I would be around 14 at the time when I was first introduced to a completely natural, yet revolutionary new float making material. Dad and I had just finished a day's fishing on the Runcorn arm of the Bridgewater canal and were heading back to dad's Llambretta scooter when we recognized a couple of anglers fishing alongside the Astmoor tannery.

Ginger Pennington and Billy Hughes, a former National Champion, were not casting the almost obligatory stick float to the far bank, they were using something completely different, and furthermore, they were catching a fish almost every cast.

This was to be my introduction to the peacock waggler, its' construction being simplicity itself. Glued into the bottom of a length of the quill was a small piece of cane around which was wrapped a spiral of lead wire. This was then attached to the line using a small piece of bicycle valve rubber, a single dust shot being the only weight on the line.

My overly fertile mind went into overdrive, and sure enough, I was much too sick to go to school the next day. Instead, I was sat on the Bridgey at Boothstown, having bought a couple of full-length peacock quills from the local tackle shop, and had assembled a "waggler" (they were not yet named) on the banking.

The float's evolution moved along rapidly, the cane and lead spiral being replaced by a hand-filed piece of brass shaped to fit into the peacock, and once again attached to the line by a length of bicycle valve rubber.

The following Friday found me sat in Benny Ashurst's kitchen with my new super float. Benny was already on the case and explained to me how the line had to be sunk to avoid surface drift, and why it was necessary to attach the float by way of a ring and not valve rubber.

"Tha strikes up wit waggler young un, not sideways," he said. "Tha'll just keep cuttin thi valve rubber, so tha must whip a ring on't bottom of't float.

Was it Benny who named the waggler; it was certainly the first time I had ever heard the word mentioned?

How lucky could a kid get with such a mentor?

* * * * *

It would be around 10 in the morning as I sat in the Hinckley offices of British Gas when the phone rang.

This was a welcome event because as per usual, boredom was setting in, and as per usual, I was doodling, drawing up plans for this super fishery I was dreaming of creating in the future - all I needed was a dustbin full of money and I would be on my way.

I had been employed by the nationalized industry for around 6 years by this time and was still waiting to find something to do, knowing full well that any form of work was strictly against union rules and could lead to instant dismissal.

The phone call lead to the commercial production of the Billy Makin Canal Grey float, a set of 5 floats that literally sold in their millions, their slim balsa construction ensuring a lifespan of seconds in many cases. These floats had to be treated with the care and reverence usually reserved when handling explosives, as one false move spelt disaster and ensured that no matter how many the angler bought, it was never enough to cover breakages.

It was often said that Mr Coleman made his fortune from the mustard left on the side of the plate after a meal, and I would guess that the majority of my float sales followed similar lines.

I could have used a stronger, heavier grade of balsa, but the balance of the float would have been affected and anglers would have only needed one of each size instead of the dozens of replacements bought every week.

Built-in obsolescence had just been invented in the fishing tackle trade.

I can well remember the day that Peter Drennon phoned to inform me that he was going to produce a float similar to my Canal Greys and simply call them Greys. I had mixed feelings at the time but had to accept that neither the word canal nor grey could be patented nor copyrighted and admired Peter for his honesty. I believe that Middy also produced a similar grey canal float shortly after, and of course, the much later formed Image company went on to produce a shorter yet highly popular model.

From such humble beginnings, new patterns of floats began to evolve, many of them variations on the original peacock theme; little changed from the peacock wagglers that I had first seen used by Ginger and Billy at Runcorn all those years earlier.

Straight peacock wagglers led to inserted, loaded, and bodied floats, all the peacock tail feathers being bought from India in their hundreds of thousands and ending up in my Hinckley factory.

I often had visions of peacocks roaming the Indian streets pursued by blokes intent on giving them sore bums, when in reality, the male birds shed their tail feathers annually.

A BUM FULL OF WAGGLERS

I began to feel a change in the air.

Swim feeders were beginning to make their presence felt, their exponentially increased use turning mediocre swims into match winners, more often than not outscoring the stick floats that I was now making.

Pole floats were being imported from Italy as more and more matchmen forsook their Canal Greys and wagglers in favour of this ever-growing new style of fishing.

My mind began to wander.

Wander back to my boring days at British Gas, as I had passed the time doodling and drawing up plans for this super fishery of the future - a fishery designed by an angler for anglers - a fishery with easy access, safe parking, toilets, and hot food.

A fishery that guaranteed that all 4 wheels would still be on your car when you returned.

It was time to stop daydreaming.

It was time to move on and build that fishery.

CHAPTER 6

A MIGHTY BREAM

The swim was good, the weather not so.

I was around 15 years old and drawn on the deep drop at Carr Mill Dam close to St Helens, where following a sharp overnight frost, the entire lake was fringed by a thin skim of ice around the margins, and we were magically surrounded by a white, picturesque, chocolate-box landscape.

Great for a man with an easel and a few dabs of paint but a looming disaster for fishermen.

The occasion was the weekly St Helens anglers Sunday match, always a 100 peg sell out, and on this icy cold day it was obvious that little more than ounces would be needed to frame, possibly even win.

Drawn next to me was dad, and unknowingly, we were sat in what in future years were to become the two most famous swims in Lancashire.

We had only discovered the Dam that Summer and armed with what at the time was perhaps a slight technological advantage, I had enjoyed a successful run of match results.

How can you describe a wooden match rod and an Alcocks

Ariel centrepin reel as advantageous technology you may well ask? Everyone had something similar, in fact, most of the other anglers had upgraded to fixed spool reels and I had been the only angler who had stuck with the centrepin for the entire Summer and Autumn.

My technology was a little more subtle than that; I had my Harry Settle float and bread punch, and when coupled with cord en bleu annatto pinkies and specials, I was the only one equipped with a gun in a knife fight.

*****

Four days earlier, as was my normal Thursday routine, I had got up early to read the Angling Times the moment it was shoved through our letterbox and something caught my eye.

There was an article about some new-fangled device invented by a chap called Jack Clayton, that despite much secrecy had escaped into the public domain.

This device was called a swing tip and had been responsible for some mighty catches of bream in the fens during the previous summer.

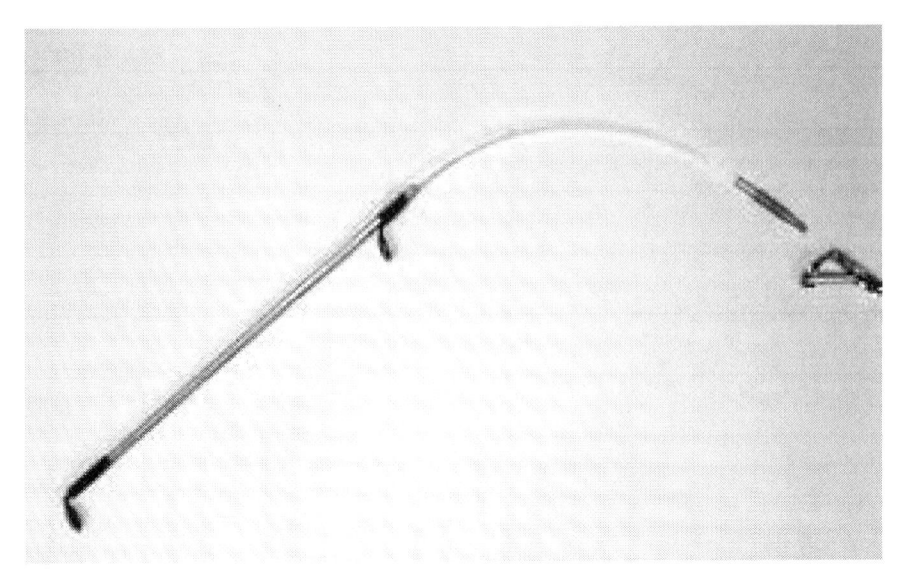

AN EARLY COMMERCIAL SWINGTIP

My fertile, some would say obsessive teenage mind kicked into gear, and throughout the day, nothing being taught in the school classroom entered my head, instead, this darn swing tip thingy would not leave me alone.

"Why just bream?" I wondered. There were many occasions when the tow on the local canals was too great to allow our newly invented wagglers to operate properly and dragging a caster along the far bank of the canal too quickly simply wasn't an option.

What if I could create a swing tip that was so sensitive that even bites from the notoriously canny Bridgewater canal roach bites could be detected?

I doodled all day long, drawing up many options from a variety of ideas until eventually, I fixed on not just the tip itself, but a method of attaching it to my rod.

That evening, Mum noticed that one of her knitting needles had disappeared, and dad noticed that I was doing a bit of work on his semi redundant tank aerial pike rod.

Yes, you read that right. There were few fibreglass and no carbon-fibre rods in those days, redundant second world war tank-aerials were often converted into pike or sea rods.

I moved back the end ring of the rod one inch and slipped on a two-inch length of bicycle valve rubber into which the newly painted 9-inch length of knitting needle was inserted, complete with end ring; I was now ready to rumble.

*****

Back at the Dam, I knew that to set up my normal wooden match rod and Harry Settle float would mean several hours of inactivity; besides, I had to test out this new-fangled swing tip thingy.

Dad looked on in amazement as I set up my new creation and attached it to his stiff-tank aerial pike rod, before bursting out laughing.

Anglers from either side also laughed as they examined what they originally thought was a broken rod.

I had been having such a good run of results all season on the Dam, so why would I want to fish with a pike rod that seemingly had the end broken off and re-attached by a two-inch piece of bicycle valve rubber?

A few hours later, our St Helens' world was to change for ever.

* * * * *

The whistle sounded, and out flew my gear on the freezing cold morning at Carr Mill Dam.

It didn't fly very far, in fact, it landed with an almighty splash at my feet.

My homemade swing tip attached to dad's pike rod had a design fault. It had a homemade fuse wire ring at one end and no ring at the other end, the end where it was attached to the rod by the valve rubber.

Several attempts later, the half-ounce bullet lead finally found its target, and I, in turn, learned to adapt by casting with a pendulum action rather than the snappier waggler type of cast.

Now came problem number 2, reaching the casting distance with my groundbait. Fortunately, I had a pretty good throwing arm as there were no groundbait catapults in those days, all bait had to be thrown in by hand - NFA rules.

Out flew half a dozen tightly squeezed tennis ball size balls of white crumb containing as many squatts as I could pack in without them disintegrating in mid-air.

After a couple of hours fishing, no one around me had caught; I however had reeled in several times to find that my single maggot bait had been crushed without any form of registration on the swing tip.

The terminal set up consisted of a half-ounce round bullet lead, through which the line was directly threaded and stopped by a bb shot, and as the lake only contained small roach, nothing registered.

Around the 3-hour mark, the tip finally showed a little life, before straightening out - slowly - ever so slowly.

Forgetting that I was using a stiff tank-aerial pike rod, I struck like a lunatic, feeling no resistance whatsoever, the resulting breakage being inevitable.

"What tha do that for Billy?" Said dad, who was now stood behind me, trying to figure out why none of the bites had been registering.

I resisted swearing as a smack round the head would have definitely been on the cards.

I re-tackled and using the exact same terminal rig, cast out once again.

I pretty much knew that I had blown my chances, and glumly stared at the motionless swing tip, when suddenly, after a couple of twitches, slowly - very slowly, it once again straightened.

This time I was under control and gently lifted the rod.

History was about to be made; Carr Mill Dam history that is.

"Fast on't bottom Billy?" said dad, who was still stood behind me.

"Yea." I replied." But it was definitely a bite."

The tank-aerial pike rod suddenly burst into life, and the Intrepid Envoy reel began to backwind.

"It's a fish dad," I said excitedly and perhaps a little too loudly. "I'm running out of line, my reel's almost empty."

In the still, icy, Carr Mill Dam air, my excited voice echoed and reverberated around the lake.

Ears pricked up.

No one back winded at Carr Mill Dam, there was nothing in the lake big enough to take line.

Not one single fish within 100 yards either side of me had been caught, and soon, a moderately interested gallery began to form behind me.

With no more than a couple of yards of line left on the reel, the fish stopped in its' tracks, turned, reluctantly gave a little ground, and began shaking its head, each thump speeding up my already racing heartbeat.

I can remember suddenly feeling very cold - trembling.

I felt uncomfortable with so many people behind me.

What if I lost it?

What was it?

Bit by bit I gained line, half a turn, occasionally one full turn of the reel handle.

This was taking for ever and I honestly began wishing that I had stayed at home that morning.

There was a collective gasp from behind me - some 30 plus anglers were now stood on the high bank looking down on me.

They could see what I couldn't - the sun was in my eyes. That is why the swims have forever been called the Sunnies.

I froze.

Lying meekly in submission in front of me was the biggest dustbin lid sized slab of a bream in the world.

I grabbed my landing net.

"Ooowed on a bit Billy." said dad. "Thas not gooin to get that thing in theeeer."

He dashed back to his swim next door, grabbed his much bigger landing net and brought it over.

WAY TOO BIG FOR MY LANDING NET

Virtually every one of the 99 anglers gathered behind me for the weigh-in that day.

No-one had ever seen a bream of this size before - there were none in Lancashire, certainly not in Carr Mill Dam.

Anything over a pound was a headline fish.

The resulting publicity in the Lancashire press was unprecedented.

For me, the bream was of considerably lesser importance than the many crushed maggots that I had experienced throughout the match.

The thirty or so unseen bites were more than the entire 99 other float fishing anglers had received in total.

I was onto something with this swing tip thingy.

OK, so how big was the biggest bream in the world that I had just landed?

Well, no one really knows, nor will they ever do. It was too big to fit in the aluminium scales pan, and as the highest weight in the match was 6 ounces, it didn't matter.

No one had ever seen a bream bigger than a couple of pounds, so estimates varied from 6 pounds up to double figures.

* * * * *

As I now had a few bob in my pocket from the match I decided to get serious about this swing tip fishing, there was definitely something to it that intrigued me.

How had I managed 30 unseen bites when few people in the match had even had one?

Why weren't there 30 fish in my net?

I checked out the local tackle shop and found a cracking 8ft fibre glass light spinning rod that was perfect for the job and spent the rest of the match money on a Mitchell 301.

WHAT AN UPGRADE – A ROLLS ROYCE OF REELS

I then shortened the homemade swing tip by a couple of inches and whipped on another ring in order to stop the tangles during casting.

Everything this end was now perfect - it was the business end that troubled me - something was drastically wrong.

The answer was serendipity, one of those "right place right time moments" that occasionally come along and have to be eagerly grasped when they do.

* * * * *

It was now Friday, and as I climbed off dad's lambretta scooter there came the unmistakable voice of the man himself.

"Ey, young Billy, come int kitchen and get waaarm, I want a word wi thi."

We were at Benny Ashurst's house collecting our bait for the weekend, and I was now sat in his kitchen having a cup of tea and explaining how I had caught the biggest bream in the world.

The papers had made a meal of it, their focus being that it had been too big for the scales; one of them had headlined me as "The Boy with the Golden Arm."

The name stuck for the rest of the time that I fished up't North, fortunately, it didn't travel down to the Midlands with me.

Like me, Benny was more interested in the bites that I hadn't seen than he was with the bream.

"Show me thi set up Billy," he said, passing over a piece of paper and a pencil.

Benny shook his head as he looked down on my sketch; he smiled and spoke.

"Thas dooin it all wrong young un, this is how tha does it."

He then drew up a simple paternoster rig, explaining how the length of the tail had to be varied depending on the bites and the fish species. "Short for roach, long for bream." He said.

"Tha doesn't want a bullet lead either young un, tha needs an arsy (Arlesey) bomb.

He went on to explain how the feeding pattern should be.

My head was spinning.

I was sat with one of the 2 greatest match anglers in the country, probably the world, and over 30 years of match fishing experience was being loaded into my 15-year-old brain - I thought it would explode.

* * * * *

It would be a little over a decade later that I was to be sat with the man who had taken over the mantle of the countries' greatest angler.

There were still a couple of empty drawers in my brain - the man from Leicester helped to fill them, but that is another story.

* * * * *

I was off to Carr Mill Dam in a couple of days.

I now had the tackle, the bait, and 30 years of unparalleled angling knowledge swirling around between my 15-year-old ears.

They were going to be in trouble up't Dam that's for sure - Benny had said so.

Dad and I thanked Benny for the cup of tea and climbed aboard the scooter, me clutching a couple of precious items from Benny's tackle box, and my schoolboy brain now filled with enough ledgering knowledge to take on the world.

Benny could talk for hours about fishing and I was quite happy to spend hours listening to one of the greatest anglers and angling brains of his generation.

"Don't use that white groundbait young un, it clags, and can sit on't bottom like a ball o dough." He then gave me a bag of brown crumb.

"Only feed once when it's coowd, never top up unless its solid and goes quiet for a spell, and then, feed very lightly."

"When thi bomb hits bottom, count to five and then pull it toward thi, that way thell have a straight line from't lead to bait. If tha's roach fishin, tha doesn't want thi maggot sittin on top of thi lead, tha'll never see a bite that way."

Just for the record, how many anglers know this, and do in fact straighten out their terminal tackle?

* * * * *

Sunday morning, freezing my goolies off, I climbed off dad's scooter to be met by "Ey up, it's little Billy Golden Arm."

I hadn't been the only one to have read the article, and when my much-acclaimed drawing hand pulled out exactly the same peg as the previous week, you can imagine the golden arm comments that followed.

As the starting whistle sounded, 99 anglers cast out their floats, and little Billy Golden Arm cast out one of Benny's "Arsy" bombs.

Four straight wins later people were beginning to take notice, and on a freezing February morning at Carr Mill Dam, 70 anglers cast out their floats, and 30 anglers cast out various leads, coupled with homemade swing tips and a mixed collection of ledgering rods that had been cobbled together.

Week eight saw the last day of the season, and by now more than half the field was on their homemade versions of the swing tip.

Dad drew Hollinhead bay, and using the light spinning rod and Mitchel 301 that I had bought him, together with the swing tip that I had made for him, he broke my winning sequence by snaring a couple of slabs.

It now became obvious that Carr Mill Dam contained more than one lonely bream.

"About time I beat thi." He said as we walked back to the scooter.

"Don't get too excited," I replied. "It won't happen again."

I got such a clout at the back of my head that I nearly fell over.

Things were different then; today he would probably be charged with attempted murder.

"Nobody likes a big head," Dad said.

He was right of course.

I was still a kid and had a lot to learn about life.

CHAPTER 7

HANDS OFF DAD

This was to be my first ever fishing holiday.

Dad and mum had booked into an old farmhouse in Wales at a little village called Arddleen, somewhere close to LLanymynech, right alongside a long-abandoned arm of the Shropshire Union canal.

I didn't catch anything during that week, I was to be born some 3 months later, so the time would be July 1949.

Every year for the next 15, this was to be the site of our family holiday, and as I got older the holiday extended to 2 weeks.

These 2-week periods every year were the happiest times of my life.

I was away from the dirt and grime of our Lancashire coal mining village. I was no longer woken by the clanking of railway coal wagons on the shunting line that ran alongside our house, instead, the morning air, so fresh that you could taste it, was filled with the sound of birds.

I remember that the sun always shone, it never rained in Arddleen, and the single-track railway was the present-day equivalent of a city bus journey for the largely farming community.

It wasn't easy making our way to Arddleen and involved multiple train and bus journeys during the early years of my life, but around the age of 8, a local tackle dealer called Len Perrin, who owned a shooting brake car, began to take us and life became much easier as by now I had a younger sister.

On one occasion Len brought along his son, Tony, who by then had begun to work in the fishing tackle trade even though he wasn't particularly interested in fishing - more about Tony later.

At the front of the old farmhouse was a large orchard with a couple of cows roaming round; they provided the milk for our tea and cornflakes, and directly in front of the gate to the orchard was what was surely the biggest tree in the world.

This tree always intrigued me, and one day when I was about 8, I resolved to climb to the very summit to check out a crow's nest.

I made it perhaps two-thirds of the way up, but on looking down, I froze. I couldn't move a muscle and flung my arms around the tree, clinging on for dear life for much of the day, by which time the entire farmhouse was out looking for me.

It was getting dark when I finally plucked up enough courage to climb down - needless to say, a fair old wallop from dad followed as mum looked on, crying with relief.

I refused to let that darn tree beat me, and every single holiday after that I climbed it just to prove that I could.

The old canal arm was badly silted up and covered in bank to bank weed, and so the day of arrival saw us all hurling various homemade dredgers tied to a length of rope to clear a swim big enough to fish.

I don't recall anyone ever catching anything other than tench, but what mighty tench they were. Every fish fought as if their very lives depended on it and tested our cane and Tonkin rods equipped with centrepin reels and 2lb line to the limit.

We landed maybe one out of every three fish that we hooked owing to the thick weed growth, but every single fish was special - I can still visualize the beautiful olive-green flanks, glinting kaleidoscope-like under the Welsh sunlight, the powerful tail and pectoral fins, and the eyes - ah yes, especially the eyes, the tiny little orange/red mesmerizing eyes that looked into your very soul with an indomitable glare of defiance.

Susanne also had beautiful eyes. Around my age, Susanne was the blonde girl who lived in the village pub and who stole my heart every year from the age of nine.

We played together in the orchard, milked the cows, went for long walks together watching the farmers load the hay and straw by pitchfork onto their trailers, we even climbed that blessed tree together - a time of wonder and innocent first love.

We ate well for those two weeks each year; Mr Roberts, the owner of the farmhouse, grew everything that we ever needed. I have to pause here awhile as I am sure that I can smell the delicious aroma of his home-cured bacon as it sizzles in the frying pan. The hams were hand-rubbed with salt and hung to cure in a pantry alongside the kitchen, and every morning, Mrs Roberts would take a carving knife and slice off the bacon for breakfast.

*****

I would be around 15 when one day I walked into Len Perrin's tackle shop close to where I lived to buy a few bits and pieces, and standing there was his son Tony, who I hadn't seen since that one holiday in Arddleen.

Tony shook my hand, which wasn't really common practice in those days, and said. "Come round the back with me Billy, I have something to show you."

We walked round to the back of the shop, Tony grabbing a rod bag and a box as we went outside. He took out the rod, pieced it together, attached the reel and handed it to me.

"Well, what do you think Billy?" He said.

I was handling my first ever glass fibre match rod and it felt good.

"Strange reel Tony," I said. "How does it work?"

"Press the black button on the top of the red casing and you are ready to cast, no more bail arm problems."

"I like the rod, Tony, it really is superb, but I'm not too sure about the reel as there is no backwind."

"Give them both a try then, they are yours now."

"WHAT?"

"As I said, they are both yours now, all you have to do is to use them for the rest of the season and let me know your views and how we can improve them."

I was now the proud yet disbelieving owner of an ABU 505 reel and an ABU Mark 5 rod.

Unknown to me at the time, Tony Perrin had been appointed marketing manager for the Swedish tackle company ABU, later becoming managing director I believe, and along with Kevin Ashurst as the angling front man for the papers, I was now acting as a sort of unpaid consultant with virtually unlimited access to all ABU products and I was still only 15.

THE GROUND-BREAKING ABU 505

It would be 2 or 3 years later that one evening, Tony came round our house in a state of unmitigated rage, tempered with despair.

"That bloody fool Ashurst." he went on. "He's bloody fired and when I get my hands on him I am going to wring his neck."

Now at the time, Tony was using Kevin as the lead man in an Angling Times marketing campaign for the ABU 505 reel, and hardly a week went by without a paid-for ad showing Kevin using his 505.

Two days earlier, Kevin had won the first-ever Woodbine final at Coombe Abbey lake with what at the time was an enormous net of bream using a Mitchell reel, and Tony had just found out that the Mitchell marketing team had got hold of the photographs.

Sure enough, that week's Angling Times had a full-page ad, complete with photographs, congratulating Kevin on his wonderful win using a Mitchell reel.

I'm not too sure how the next meeting between Tony and Kevin went, but I would have loved to have been a fly on the wall that day.

I suppose that it would have been perhaps 3 years after first receiving my ABU rod and reel that Tony popped round to our little terraced miner's house with the first ABU Mark 6 rod and 506 reel in the country.

Dad was well pleased - he was to finally get his hands on my jealously guarded Mark 5 rod and my 505 reel.

* * * * *

Important things rods, some of them, despite feeling good, simply don't work for certain types of fishing, the most perfect example being the old carbon fibre Shakespeare President.

It may have been adequate for river fishing, but for canal work, it was an absolute disaster, the spliced solid carbon fibre tip producing a "knocking" effect as the hollow section came into play, resulting in small fish being bounced off the hook.

At the time, the technology wasn't available to produce hollow carbon fibre tips, so Bruce and Walker took a different route, solving the problem by using inter woven fibre glass for the end two-thirds of the top section - it worked better than the Shakespeare solution to the problem, but as the fibre glass was much heavier than its' carbon equivalent, the balance never felt quite right.

*****

Now at the time of receiving my ABU Mark 5 rod from Tony, glass fibre wasn't completely new to me as I had modified the solid glass fibre spinning rod for my early swing tipping at Carr Mill Dam.

For 3 months every year this little spinning rod saw another use.

At the time, and for another 20 years, match fishing ground to a halt owing to the 3-month closed season, and not wishing to suffer the pangs of withdrawal symptoms, every Sunday, my club, the King's Head of Bolton arranged a trip to lake Windermere in search of trout, the only method allowed being ledgered worm.

Very few fish were ever caught, and it is fair to say that if you did catch one, you would almost certainly win the 2-bob sweepstake that everyone on the coach entered.

Earlier in the book I wrote at length about Harry Settle.

Harry was on every trip and was a trickster beyond belief. If Harry moved from his seat, everyone watched him like a hawk, and the only angler brave enough to ever sit next to Harry was a giant of a man known as Alan McAtee, big Al becoming an England international in future years.

Sleeping anglers awoke with itching powder sprinkled down their shirts or around their mysteriously open fly holes, pockets contained mouse traps or stink bombs, cigarettes contained mini explosive devices. Harry delighted in such capers, and on one occasion the coach was stopped by police after breakfast at the XL transport cafe and everyone had to turn out their pockets which were found to contain knives, forks, salt and pepper pots, and bottles of various sauces, all removed by Harry from the cafe.

Now the fishing was dire, and an average of one trout per coachload every 2 trips was the norm, until someone, you will never guess who, sussed out how to win the sweepstake every week.

PRIVATE FISHING SYNDICATE MEMBERS ONLY.

At the head of Lake Windermere are two trout streams, the rivers Brathy and Rothy. Both were strictly private and reserved for fly-fishing members, and as no-one ever seemed to be around, I wandered upstream through the meadows of Spring daffodils, every bit as lonely as Wordsworth must have been, with my little glass fibre spinning rod and centrepin reel, flicking a worm into every likely hole, and just as the sun began to set returned to the rest of the party proudly displaying the biggest trout that I had landed, naturally enough not mentioning the other dozen or more fish that were hidden in my basket.

Occasionally I passed the biggest trout over to dad when no one was looking, not wishing to arouse too much suspicion.

Golden Arm had turned into a bounder, still, dad and I always had a free weekend's fishing and no one was ever any the wiser, and as was pretty much tradition, the winner always spent his winnings buying the first round on the obligatory pub stop on the way home.

In case you haven't already worked it out.

Beer was less than 2 bob a pint.

CHAPTER 8

KEVIN

"That's it, I've had enough." A young, twenty-something Kevin Ashurst slammed his rod down and stood up.

"What's up Kev?" I had already guessed the answer to the question and was having difficulty keeping a straight face.

"This bloody line that th'owd chap gave me Billy is rotten; I've had three chucks and lost three hooks on fish. I'm going to get my other reel back and strangle him."

My face wanted to laugh but my brain said no.

Should I tell him?

No, this was just too much fun and was going to get even better.

Off up the canal Kevin strode in the direction of Benny, and into his swim, right alongside the pipe gushing hot water, sailed my float.

He returned some 10 minutes later, and I resumed casting into my own swim, my keepnet now containing 5 good sized fish, all taken from the hot steaming swim that Kevin was now going to chuck into once again.

BIG KEV

* * * * *

It had been a horrible Winter, temperatures rarely rising above zero, and all fishing had ground to a halt as the Lancashire canals and lakes had a 6-inch lid of ice on them when we heard of the Hotties on the canal at St Helens.

The journey on the back of dad's Llambretta scooter had been painful as we pulled up alongside the canal for the first time, to be greeted by a friendly face from the Summer matches at Carr Mill Dam.

"Go close to the bridge Billy." Dennis had said. "Fish as close to the big outlet pipe as you can, the place is solid."

What an amazing sight was in store for us; the whole place was shrouded in steam as the hot water from the sprinklers obscured entire areas; not even a square inch of the canal past the halfway mark was visible.

Opposite the canal was the Pilkingtons' glass works, and the recycled water was used in the glass making process to cool the poured glass.

I plunged my frozen hands into the water and was tempted to do the same with my feet – it was bathwater warm.

Dad and I had found heaven – a Winter paradise.

Fish were topping everywhere, and I couldn't wait to get going.

My hands were now pink and tingling as I tackled up directly opposite the hot water pipe that was gushing a constant stream of slightly tinged, near-boiling water, that on hitting the canal produced a cloud of steam so dense that only occasionally was I able to see the actual canal.

On closer inspection it became clear that a large eddy had formed, and this spinning swirl of turbulence was an obvious target.

My waggler sailed serenely across the canal, my size 18's hook buried inside a caster.

The float dipped within seconds of hitting the water and I struck.

"Damn, must have struck too hard," I muttered as I tied on another hook.

Dad glared; I wasn't allowed to swear.

Two more casts and two more hooks later, Dennis walked up to me sporting a grin big enough to connect both of his ears.

"Having problems with the Cichlids are we Billy Boy, they always hang around this hot water pipe? Shallow up, stick on a 16's and just nick the caster or you will soon run out of hooks."

CICHLID – TOOTHY LITTLE BLIGHTERS

Mission accomplished and two minutes later I slid the net under my first British Cichlid, a fish I caught in the hundreds a few years later in Singapore during my stint in the army protecting the rapidly shrinking British Empire.

The canal was teaming with them; apparently, some pet shop owner had tipped a few tropical fish into the canal a couple of years earlier and the blighters had thrived and bred thanks to the tropical temperature of the water.

They weren't always easy to catch, and the row of small yet razor-sharp teeth, both top and bottom, meant that your line had only to brush against them and you were hookless.

I soon worked out a method of catching them based pretty much on the advice that Dennis had given me that day.

Kevin re-tackled and once again his waggler sailed into the spot that I had just been poaching, and slowly at first, the swearing began to gather momentum and volume.

Should I tell him I pondered?

No, it was now becoming absolutely hilarious.

"Stop laughing," I told myself a hundred times. "Have you seen the size of the ape-like figure that you are laughing at?" (Sorry Kev, but you are seven thousand miles away, so I reckon that I am pretty safe here in Thailand).

Kevin was on the verge of bursting a blood vessel when one of his mates stood behind him and explained the problem.

"Did tha' know about these bloody Piranhas, Billy?"

"No Kev, what do you mean?"

I couldn't contain myself any longer and nearly choked on a cup of coffee that I was drinking.

Kevin glared.

I prepared to run.

Kevin growled and tied on another hook.

* * * * *

It wasn't long after the above comedy of errors that my fragile body again succumbed to an ever-re-occurring mystery illness that always necessitated a day off school and a trip to the St Helens' Hotties.

I was on a different swim to the hot water pipe so beloved by Kevin, just below a small weir-like structure that separated the Hotties from Todds' length and was surprised to find myself catching baby cichlids no more than half an ounce each. These were tiny fish that had been washed over the weir and were now forced to live permanently in that one swim, the rest of the length being too cold for them to survive.

A strange speaking chap came and stood behind me, and told me that he was from Sheffield, which of course is on the wrong side of the Pennines.

"Do you want to sell me some of them lad?" He said. "I'll give you ten bob for every one that you catch."

At the age of fourteen, ten bob was a couple of month's pocket money for me, and if he had offered a tanner each I would still have ripped his hand off.

The following Wednesday, I was again struck by the mystery illness and had to skip school, and as the light faded, I handed over 50 tiny cichlids to the strange speaking chap from Yorkshire, and he, in turn, handed me twenty-five quid, a positive King's ransom.

The chap was a lovely bloke and told me that he was a major tropical fish dealer and received a fiver for every fish, which he then wholesaled throughout the country.

And so it was that my budding entrepreneurial career began at an early age, as every few weeks for almost 2 years, I was struck down by this mystery illness that always seemed to surface on a Wednesday.

It wasn't always plain sailing though.

Occasionally I had to go through the pain barrier while bent over the chair in the headmaster's office.

Apparently, schooldays are five days a week and are supposed to include Wednesdays.

Not for me though.

Dad earned a tenner a week at the local mine and worked seriously hard for his money, and with two kids to bring up, twenty-five quid a month, sometimes twice a month, went a long way, resulting in the Llambretta being replaced by a Reliant three-wheeler.

Winter fishing became a whole lot more fun after that.

I don't know what happened to the strange speaking chap from Sheffield, but he simply stopped phoning me, and for a while I considered putting in a five-day shift at school.

Benny soon put a stop to such silly thoughts when he began running Wednesday matches at Runcorn on the Bridgewater canal.

How I ever got to university is still a mystery, especially to the headmaster, who eventually washed his hands of me before finally expelling me for firing pouchfuls of maggots across the canal opposite the school at every passing schoolmaster on one of my Wednesdays off.

CHAPTER 9

IVAN

It would be difficult to write a series of articles covering some 30 years of match fishing without bringing to life some of the great anglers that I had the privilege of both meeting and competing against.

So far, I have included Harry Settle, Benny and Kevin Ashurst, and Alan McAtee.

Now I will resurrect perhaps the most famous of them all - Ivan Marks.

I always felt that I knew Ivan well, long before I ever met or spoke to him; an army friend of mine had a complete set of Ivan Marks floats when I was stationed in Singapore, and as dad always sent the Angling Times over, I built up a fairly comprehensive mental picture of the man, and on eventually meeting him, I wasn't disappointed.

Ivan was an icon, a mystical chain-smoking bohemian character who carried around with him an aura so intense that you could feel it before you got close.

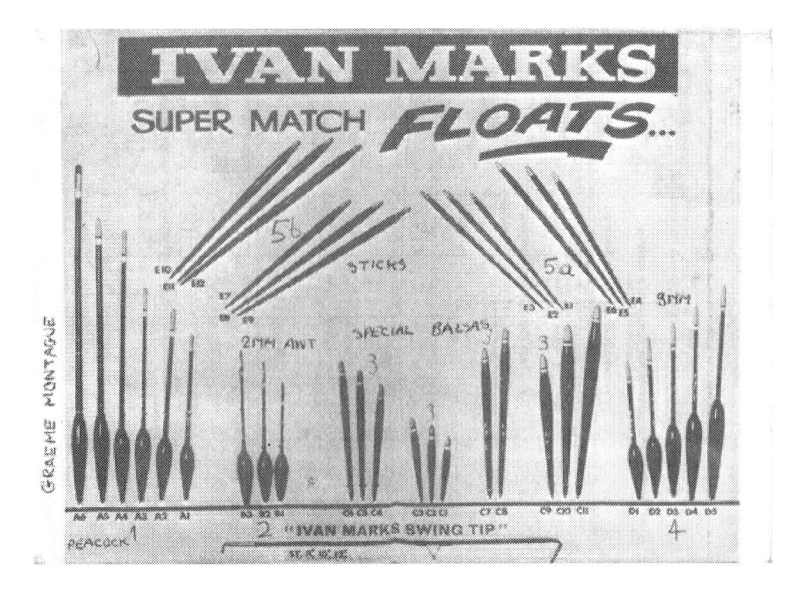

I suppose that the time would be the late 70's, the venue was Attenborough gravel pits, and the swim was number 29, smack bang in the corner of Sandy bay. The match was of course run by Steve (RIP OFF) Toone, who like Pat O'Connor, is owed a great deal of gratitude for the job that they both did in bringing to life the Midland's match circuit

Now for anyone who has never experienced the following phenomena, it will be difficult to believe and even more difficult to visualize, but the peg simply had too many fish in it, the fish in question being big, beautiful, slab-sided bream. This was in the days before carp had been invented, and before some idiot whose name was remarkably similar to mine dug a few holes in the ground and began the commercial fisheries revolution.

I kicked off the match with half a dozen orange sized balls of brown bread crumb filled with casters, followed by my Benny Ashurst inspired terminal ledger rig complete with an 18's hook and a single annatto special maggot.

Very soon I found myself in bream hell.

I was way out of my depth; every time my lead hit the water, the quiver tip went berserk, and after 2 hours I had managed 3 fish and had become a nervous, dribbling, semi-insane wreck when from over the rainbow, salvation arrived in the form of the master himself - Ivan Marks.

IVAN - SIMPLY THE BEST

Ivan sat behind me, grinning, and shaking his head in disapproval as he watched the pantomime unfold before his disbelieving eyes.

Having cut my ledgering teeth on the tiny roach at Carr Mill Dam, I was used to striking at the slightest twitch of the Quiver tip.

This is not the way to catch bream.

"For God's sake Billy," he eventually said, still shaking his head and unable to take any more. "Do you want me to show you how to catch bream?"

Obviously, no one could refuse an offer like that from the world's finest bream angler, so I nodded.

He took out of his pocket a packet of size 12's hooks and told me to tie one on and to lengthen my hook length to 5 feet. Size 12's hooks were for hanging slabs of meat on at the butchers, but I wasn't going to question the judgement of my long-time angling hero, so on it went, on went 2 worms tipped with a caster to stop them covering the point of the hook, and out into peg 29 went the lot.

Ivan stood up and broke a small whippy branch from a weeping willow tree that was growing alongside me before stripping off the leaves.

Immediately, as he sat back down on the grass beside me, the quiver tip started to dance, and as I made a grab for the rod, Ivan whacked me across the knuckles with the stick.

"Strike when I tell you to Billy," he said. "Now take your hands away from the rod and sit on them."

I now had to endure 5 minutes of torture as the quiver tip performed the bossa-nova, the twist, and the tango; I was becoming dizzy, my arms continually twitching like a rabbit's nose with every movement, and every time I reached for the rod, down came Ivan's stick onto my knuckles. Eventually, the tip went slowly round and stayed there - the reel slowly began to spin. "Lift now," Ivan said calmly, "but don't strike."

I lifted and joyously felt one of the most exciting and orgasmically pleasurable sensations that any match man can ever feel - the satisfying thump that only a good-sized slab can deliver as it shakes its head.

Carp are different. There is no mystery - no magic in a fish that simply wants to frantically bolt in whatever direction it is facing at the time.

I felt none of the trepidation or fear that had accompanied my other 3 fish that had been tenuously connected to a size 18 hook - this one was going nowhere but in my keepnet - Ivan said so.

A 4lb bream surfaced and was soon in my net, followed by several more, until at the final whistle I had 60lb instead of the 20 that I had been heading for before Ivan had delivered his masterclass.

The next day I rang in work and booked a week's holiday, and for the next 5 days, I travelled to Attenborough, always fishing peg 29, and putting into practice a lifetime of Ivan's experience in catching bream, a knowledge which I had been blessed with in no more than 3 hours.

Blow me, the next Sunday I again drew peg 29 and the Sunday after.

It seemed that I had brought my golden arm at the draw bag all the way from St Helens to Nottingham.

One of the Nottingham lads who had seen me practising for a week, and then drawing the same swim 3 weeks on the trot, remarked. "Is Toony screwing you, Billy?"

"Of course not," I replied indignantly. "But if he lets me draw peg 29 again next week, I might let him."

* * * * *

At the point where Ivan had entered the scene, I had become a wreck. My hands were trembling, and my heartbeat was well into three figures. Not only had I never caught real slab-sided bream on the canals of Lancashire, but I had also never even seen a bream of over 2 pounds other than the one-off monster at Carr Mill Dam all those years before, yet here I was sat on several hundred of the blighters and I hadn't a clue what I was doing.

I have already described the set up that Ivan advised, and on reflection, I believe that it was prescribed for two reasons, the most important of which was for my benefit and not for the fish. Ivan had to calm me down otherwise my confidence would have been totally shattered.

I NEEDED CALMING DOWN – IVAN WAS ON HAND

He did exactly the same thing with Dennis White a couple of years later in a Winter League final at Coombe Abbey. That time was well spent for the Barnsley team, as my team finished less than a couple of pounds behind them and were denied the title.

Ivan had continued to speak throughout the match, and slowly to begin with, the trembles eventually faded. Without realizing it, a succession of 4lb bream had begun to fill the keepnet and Ivan's lifetime of knowledge was beginning to fill my head.

From now on the rest of the piece is pretty much in my own words; however, you have to remember that the events were almost 40 years ago, nevertheless, the sentiments are those of the Master, and in many ways echo and endorse much of what Benny Ashurst had instilled in me. Maybe these issues had been discussed between them; strangely, a feeling of Deja vu always appeared whenever I discussed fishing with Ivan, and visions of Benny himself often appeared in my subconscious.

"Imagine spreading a few slices of bread on the garden. It may take an hour or so, but eventually, a sparrow will appear. If you disturb that sparrow, it could easily be a long time before the next one arrives - if you do not disturb it, the garden will soon be full of sparrows. Bream are just like that." Ivan had said. "Allow them to settle before you start to catch them."

Hadn't Benny said something similar?

My fertile mind travelled back many years.

* * * * *

As a lad, in our coal mining village we had what we called a "Knocker Up". This was a little old chap who went around the miner's houses, usually around 5 in the morning, and using a length of bamboo poles tied together, tapped on the miner's windows to wake them up for the early shift. When fishing, if we caught an early fish and couldn't get another bite, we used to say that we had caught the "Knocker Up".

* * * * *

Good grief - things were beginning to fall into place.

Take the "Knocker Up" out of the equation, and the miners overslept - disturb the first sparrow and the rest of the flock will not appear - catch the first bream in the swim and ----- you can finish the rest.

Think about that for a while and now go back to the canal days.

Only a fool cast out a waggler or pushed out the pole to the far bank as soon as the match began. You needed the fish to settle - you needed to build up their confidence.

YOU MOST CERTAINLY DIDN'T WANT TO CATCH THE KNOCKER UP

* * * * *

I am now back on the Attenborough peg 29 aquarium, and between my slipping the net under a series of slabs, Ivan continued to speak and told me about the ten-bite rule.

"You only ever need ten bites to win a bream match anywhere in the country," he said. "That works out at one bite every half hour."

I thought about it for a couple of minutes before re-baiting and casting out again.

"If the shoal is settled and feeding confidently, you should never miss a bite if your set up is right; you will also eliminate most of the line bites as the fish will no longer be nervously milling around."

The quiver tip twitched.

I twitched and reached for the rod.

The stick once again rapped me on the knuckles.

Ivan continued with the masterclass, and slowly, the tip swung round, and the rod began to follow it.

These bream were becoming a damned nuisance and were interrupting my concentration - I didn't want to miss a single word.

There would be many opportunities to catch bream in the future, but to receive a 3-hour lesson from the master was a once in a lifetime chance to leapfrog many years of trial and error - imagine, how many people were ever given the opportunity of picking up a lifetime's knowledge of bream fishing from Ivan Marks?

"It isn't all about size 12's hooks and double worm," he said. "Sometimes you will have to fish a single maggot on a size '20s, then it is even more important to take your time and make every bite count; confidence is the key - you have to build up the fish's confidence before you even think about catching them."

For those of you who have been privileged enough to have watched Ivan in full cry among a bream shoal, I'm sure that you will agree, he could be bloody infuriating.

He would slip the net under a slab - drop his rod on the rest - light a fag and turn around to talk to the gallery that always accompanied him, sometimes for up to 10 minutes.

This wasn't Ivan simply being Ivan as we all thought.

This was Ivan observing his 10-bite rule; he was resting his swim, after all, he only needed one bite every 30 minutes.

* * * * *

After my 3rd win at the Attenborough peg 29 aquarium, I had shot to the top of the Matchman of the Year rankings and found myself suddenly elevated to the status of an (A) lister, if such a thing could ever be ascribed to a coal miner's son and a tin of worms.

For people of more recent vintage, at the time, it appeared that a form of celebrity fishing was on the verge of taking off, in fact, I did a couple of series of Pro-Celebrity shows for ITV, and believe it or not, a well-paid TV commercial.

Every other week there was a special match, often massively supported by a sponsor, and 20 or so of the country's top anglers were invited. I had now become one of the select few. My fishing cap was becoming too small; I was having thoughts above my station.

I had done a near impossible treble in three weekends and coupled with the BBC Champions title I had just won; I was now sat at my swim on the private bank at Coombe Abbey.

All around me were magical names - Kenny - Clive - Denis - Kevin - Robin - Roy - Ian, and of course the master himself - Ivan.

When the starting whistle went my confidence suddenly evaporated.

I went into meltdown.

What on earth was I doing in such company?

Two pegs away was THE MAN himself, Ivan.

Why had I so stupidly wasted a day's holiday from British Gas? I was in much too far over my depth.

I knew how a drowning man felt.

SELF DOUBT SET IN

I took a deep breath.

Reality kicked in.

Two whole lifetimes of unparalleled match fishing genius and knowledge had been squeezed into my eagerly receptive brain by both Benny Ashurst and Ivan Marks.

No one else on the banking that day had been tutored by the two greatest anglers of their generation.

Ivan's words kept resonating around my brain, and Benny's invaluable advice flashed before my eyes.

My confidence returned and I began to feel better.

For 5 amazing hours, Ivan and I matched each other fish for fish.

The scales decided the outcome.

Ivan's 10 slabs weighed 48lb and my 10 magically topped them by 4 ounces.

Ivan's ten bite rule had only been partially correct.

At the presentation, I floated on air as I collected my cheque for 1,000 pound.

There are no prizes for guessing who the first man was to congratulate me.

Ivan not only shook my hand, but he put his arm around me in the most genuine gesture of affection I have ever seen.

I would have willingly ripped the cheque into a thousand pieces if I could have only frozen that priceless moment in time.

*****

Another great angler I was proud to call my friend was Dave Berrows.

I have moved on a few years and was sat on the Trent and Mersey canal somewhere in Staffordshire.

This was Dave Berrows' country and winning a match in this part of the world was as easy as falling off a log - you simply had to catch one more fish than Berrowsy.

DAVE BERROWS – CANAL ANGLER SUPREME

Dave had drawn well in a noted gudgeon area and was odds on.

My swim wasn't so good but occasionally threw up an odd decent caster roach.

To my right across the canal was a fishy little bush, and I fired an odd caster over for the first half-hour as I scratched around for a few gudgeon. I then pushed over the long pole and slipped the net under a decent roach.

Now was decision time?

Ivan's masterclass 10 bite rule flashed before me.

Did it only work for bream or were there wider applications of the master's philosophy?

How many of you would have immediately pushed out the pole again?

I suspect almost everyone - I didn't - I had been to the master class.

Throughout the entire match I only pushed it across a dozen times.

I got my ten caster bites.

As for Dave Berrows?

Quite obviously massively overrated - I had annihilated him by almost half an ounce in his own back garden with just a little assistance from the master himself.

I believe that Dave became a broken man and took up knitting and yoga before going into therapy shortly afterwards.

CHAPTER 10

THE FIN

Before the building of Makin Fisheries, I had a small factory at Hinckley where I turned out a million floats a year, many of which were exported to the continent, the majority however being funnelled through a series of UK wholesalers and van men.

One such van man was Neil Higginson, a successful angler on the Warwickshire Avon circuit.

One day, Neil called round the factory to pick up an order and asked if I fancied popping over to Coventry to the Angling Trades Association (ATA) show.

I jumped in Neil's van and some 30 minutes later we walked into the hotel hosting the show, which is done for the benefit of the tackle trade and not the angler. These tackle shows were usually conducted in early Spring to allow the manufacturers or wholesalers to showcase their new lines of tackle for the shops to order in time for the Summer months, which naturally enough is the time when most anglers go fishing.

Things looked quite impressive with most of the big boys and their sales teams' present, their stalls well-lit and well laid out, the salesmen eager to demonstrate their new products and to steal an edge over their competitors.

Right by the door was someone I didn't recognize; a quiet, studious sort of fellow who I thought looked a little like an Indian, and in front of him was a small folding table, sitting on which was 4 pieces of plastic.

DAVE PRESTON – STILL LOOKS LIKE AN INDIAN TO ME

As you can imagine, this little folding table looked pretty much out of place among the glamorous displays of the Daiwa's, Shimano's, and Shakespeare's of this world and I couldn't help wondering what on earth he was doing there.

Neil and I were intrigued, and after introductions, I asked the chap what exactly were these 4 little pieces of plastic that he was displaying? The unexpected reply was that they were feet for the Octoplus seat box to stop the rather thin legs of the box from sinking into the mud.

Neil and I looked at each other a little sympathetically and moved on to the big stands, thinking little about his display.

It would be around 3 months later that I noticed a piece about a well-made PTFE pole bush in the angling press, the name behind the bush being a certain Dave Preston, the name I recognized from the ATA show with his 4 plastic feet.

The rest of course is history, the name Preston Innovations now being synonymous with much of the finest match fishing tackle available both in the UK and across the continent.

Dave and I became good friends and in later years worked together in promoting our products to the angler, however, the business side of the fishery relationship had a rather strange beginning.

* * * * *

From day one of Makin Fisheries, by a process of pleading, grovelling, and finally blackmail, I managed to secure sponsorship of the lakes by Daiwa thanks to John Middleton, the M.D. of Daiwa UK.

John and I had a good relationship for several years, and as the fishery grew, so did the sponsorship figure, however, a dark cloud one day appeared on the horizon in the form of several batty individuals calling themselves the Barbel Society.

"Barbel are river fish and will not survive in still waters." I was constantly told.

Being the first to stock barbel into still waters, I became a target, even though not only did the fish survive, but they also positively thrived, growing at more than double the rate of their river brethren.

As their objections had little effect on the stubborn individual that I am, they turned their attention to John and Daiwa, threatening to arrange a boycott of all Daiwa tackle.

John gave way, and I have to say that in his position representing such a prestigious company, I would probably have done the same.

Up stepped Dave Preston, who by now was making much more than plastic feet and seeing the obvious promotional possibilities of his company's association with what had now grown into Europe's biggest commercial fishery, handed over a nice fat cheque worth many times the amount that Daiwa had been paying.

MAKIN FISHERIES WITH NEW SPONSOR

Thank you, you batty individuals of the barbel society.

It is noticeable that virtually every commercial fishery now successfully stock their lakes with barbel, a gift that just keeps on giving.

As the demands on my time grew, I eventually closed my float factory, selling the equipment to none other than Dave Preston, and a little later arranged a meeting at his Telford factory, taking along with me a certain rather shy chap called Andy Findlay.

*****

Andy had been brought to my attention by Terry, my fishery manager, and was still pretty much unknown on the open match circuit.

"You have got to watch this guy," Terry had said. "He's virtually unbeatable."

I watched him one day as he was pleasure fishing Reptile pool on Phase 2 of the lakes, and Terry was right. With me that day was a fellow called Bob Nudd, who during the morning had just completed a feature for the Angling Times.

We both sat in silence behind Andy for some 20 minutes before Bob spoke.

"Don't ever let this fellow come down South to my circuit Billy," Bob said. "He will destroy it."

I had seen enough - the 4 times world champion was right.

THE FIN – A LEGEND IN THE MAKING

Now the reason why I had taken Andy along to meet Dave Preston was that having watched him fish, I knew that very soon sponsors would be queueing up for his signature, and to complete the circle of Preston Innovations, Makin Fisheries and Andy Findlay was the dream ticket.

After introducing Andy to Dave Preston, the three of us were accompanied by Rickie Teale, Dave's right-hand man, as we went upstairs in the factory to view the still-secret new range of rods that were due to hit the market within the next few weeks.

We all stood back as Andy took each rod in turn, flexed it, waggled it, then asked Rickie to hold the end as he examined both the torque and the curve profile.

I gasped in horror as Andy then pronounced the entire range as "Pretty Crap."

"Cancel the lot, Rickie," Dave said. "We'll start again."

It was now Rickie's turn to gasp in horror.

Andy and Rickie then spent the next hour going through the entire range.

Details of the necessary modifications were urgently sent to China that very same day.

Two weeks later, Andy and I walked into the Preston Innovations' factory to be greeted by a grinning Rickie Teale.

"He was spot on Billy," Rickie said. "Come and try these out."

A few weeks later, the finest ledger and feeder rods ever made hit the UK market.

Needless to say, Andy got his sponsorship deal and went on to design some of Preston Innovations' most innovative innovations.

CHAPTER 11

STEVIE

I think that I may have been on the Thames, perhaps somewhere around Oxford, as I talked to Kenny Collins.

Around this time, Kenny, Keith Arthur, and a chap called Stevie Gardner were beginning to establish dominance on the lower river with superb bags of dace, and the Angling Times were devoting many column inches to the three anglers, particular Stevie.

KEITH ARTHUR – MATCHMAN AND TV PERSONALITY

"How good is he Kenny?" I asked, as together with Keith, we walked down the riverbank to our swims one day; I had never met Stevie nor had I seen him fish. "Can you beat him?"

"If we both start on the right method, I can hold my own with him." He continued. "If things have changed, however, you can guarantee that Stevie will be the first one in the match to sort it out."

Keith nodded in agreement.

* * * * *

It was a few years later and I was somewhere down South, my head forlornly resting in my hands wondering why I had accepted the invitation to fish what was a pretty big money match on a peggy little river.

"Bring some proper tackle," I had been told. "And plenty of casters, the river is chocka with big chub and barbel."

I was on the upper reaches of the River Lea staring at what was probably the worst peg I had ever drawn in my life if big fish were to be the target.

The swim was bank to bank with luxuriant, thick streamer weed, with a narrow channel, perhaps one yard wide down the middle.

I had brought some proper tackle.

I had size 16's hooks and 3lb line, enough to tie up a battleship in those pre- carp days, but to have banked a frisky gudgeon from the jungle in front of me would have been difficult, never mind a chub or barbel.

Stevie Gardner and his friend walked up and stood behind me, both sporting big grins.

STEVIE – THE FINEST INTERNATIONAL NEVER
TO BECOME WORLD CHAMPION

"What the heck am I supposed to do here Stevie?" I asked.

"You could try praying," came the not unexpected reply, and with that, they both disappeared downstream still grinning.

Some 10 minutes later Stevie returned shaking his head in disbelief.

"Fancy swapping pegs Billy?" he said. "Come and look at mine."

I didn't grin on arriving at Stevie's swim; I burst out laughing and can still visualize every detail some 30 years later.

This really was the worst swim ever pegged in the history of match fishing.

Not only was it narrow, but it was also little more than inches deep, and perhaps 5 yards downstream the water almost disappeared as it tumbled over and through an impassable gravel and rock bed, so drawing fish from downstream was out of the question as they simply couldn't have physically swum through the inch deep barrier.

Making matters even worse was the low, crystal clear water conditions, and if so much as a minnow had been in the swim it would have been visible.

To this day, I will stake my miserable life on the peg being devoid of all fish life, it really was that bad.

The thought of even tackling up would never have crossed my mind - why bother? The swim was not only barren, but it was also pretty much unfishable because of the depth, the funniest part of all being the fact that one of the world's best anglers was sat on it.

He wasn't grinning now - he who laughs last.

"Fancy a fiver as a side bet Stevie," I said hopefully.

I can't quite remember his reply, but I guess that when

translated into the Queen's Lancashire it would have probably meant no.

I returned to my swim still chuckling to myself and got ready for the off.

The little channel between the streamer weed was around 3 feet deep, and I had decided that to fish with the 3lb boat rope and 16's hook was silly and offered no advantage whatsoever, as landing a chub or a barbel would have been impossible.

Still, under such low water conditions, and on a crystal-clear river, it was possible that the big fish would not feed, so, I would go for the only things that it was possible to land, confident that looking so fishy it would be full of small roach and dace among the dense streamer weed.

Down sailed the stick float with a 1lb hook length and a single caster on a size '20s, and 10 pegs below me, a rather silly man answering to the name of Stevie Gardner foolishly did something similar.

What happened later that day was one of the most remarkable and unbelievable fishing events and performances that I have ever witnessed in my life.

My stick float sailed majestically down the River Lea, uninterrupted by anything with scales on for well over an hour.

A cheesed off angler came walking down river and informed me that no one above me had caught a single fish.

This actually cheered me up as I had a 30-yard swim all to myself, and surely there had to be something somewhere? It was just a matter of time.

*****

I was now 2 hours into the match and still fishless when Stevie's mate, the one who had been grinning at my swim before the start, came and stood behind me.

"Stevie would like a few casters," he said. "Have you got any to spare?"

"You can take the flippin lot as far as I'm concerned," I replied. "There are 5 pints in the bag behind me and bugger all in the river in front of me."

I was of course joking. There was no way that Stevie needed any bait and quite obviously his mate was joking as well.

Without saying another word, the plonker then picked up my bag containing the 5 pints of casters and disappeared downstream with it.

FIVE FLIPPIN PINTS – STILL NOT PAID ME

When I realized what had happened, I lay down my rod and

set off after him; I needed those casters for the Monday sweepstake at Mallory Park. I caught up with him 10 pegs downstream sat behind Stevie, who was just in the process of bursting open one of my bags of casters.

"Thanks for the bait Billy," Stevie said. "Watch this, you won't believe it."

I looked out into the still barren swim in front of him and noticed that his keepnet was staked out a third of the way across the river in some 3 inches of water, and in the net I could see what appeared to be a few dorsal fins.

Surely not.

Stevie then angled himself to his left and fired in more casters than I had used in the previous 2 hours alongside a small bush, some 3 or 4 yards upstream.

A DARK SHADOW MOVED DOWN STREAM AND WITHIN SECONDS WAS DIRECTLY IN FRONT OF HIM

He did nothing.

The shadow moved on downstream.

I gasped - the shadow was an enormous shoal of chub, all of which were following Stevie's (my) casters downstream, gobbling up everything in sight.

On reaching the one-inch-deep gravel and rock barrier, they all turned around and headed back towards their home, this being the bush a few yards upstream of Stevie.

Stevie was poised for action.

Over went a small stick float, almost scraping the gravel bottom of the swim.

This was where the genius known as Stevie Gardner was now displayed for all to see.

The float was set some 2 feet deep in no more than a few inches of water, and as far as I could see there was no shot on the line.

Stevie mended the line, held back the float, and his double caster moved in front of the float and broke the surface.

The swim was so shallow and so clear that I could see each individual caster.

As the shoal moved back into range, he released the brake on the float and the double caster sailed serenely into the mouth of the leading chub.

This was so simple.

It was so blindingly obvious that a chimpanzee could have worked it out.

World-class anglers make everything look simple.

I was witnessing one of the best anglers in the world at the peak of his powers.

For the next 2 hours, I was privileged to watch the finest angling performance
that it has ever been my good fortune to see.

Almost all my 5 pints of casters were put to good use.

Any ideas as to what finally finished up in Stevie's keepnet?

Try one hundred pounds and you will still be well short.

This on a small river, inches deep, with absolutely -- NO -- fish whatsoever in the swim.

Stevie Gardner was the finest International angler never to have become an individual world champion.

Does anyone disagree?

For a Southern woofter, he could fish a bit could Stevie.

And just for the record, 30 years later, I am still awaiting the 20 quid that he promised me for the casters.

* * * * *

Now we Northerners are not so mean.

Margaret, Ian Heaps' wife, walked across the manicured lawns of Woburn Abbey one bright Summer's day during a reasonably sized match and stood behind me chatting before offering a similar request for casters, telling me that Ian was emptying the big lake.

I gave her the 4 surplus pints that I had brought in the hope of drawing a bream swim, and one hour later saw me sat behind the Stockport maestro as he slipped the net under a succession of slabs.

"Margaret agreed 20 quid." I jokingly said as a marauding carp crashed through his swim.

Ian grinned as he slipped his landing net under the beast.

IAN HEAPS – NOT MEAN AT ALL

At the presentation, he slipped me 40 quid out of his winnings.

Both Stevie and Ian were two anglers that I was privileged to know and fish with, Ian becoming a world champion - an accolade unjustly denied to Stevie.

In my splendid isolation over here in Thailand, I know little of today's anglers, but if they are half as interesting and inspiring as the true greats of the sport that I fished with during the Golden Age of Match Fishing, then they are indeed very lucky.

CHAPTER 12

AS THE MILLER TOLD HIS TALE

It's a funny old thing is the human brain.

How come that having swallowed my last mouthful of bacon butty in the morning, ten minutes later I find myself wondering what I will have for breakfast?

On the other hand, occasionally something crops up, and a memory that has remained dormant for near 50 years suddenly appears with such alarming clarity that I can be transported back in time and find myself a young man once again, directly involved in the events that unfolded at the time.

Not many people have this ability, and near-total recall becomes more and more elusive as age sets in. In my case, however, I can often drift back to a bygone age, the images being so clear that I can actually hear the words spoken at the time, or even more satisfying, see the float disappear, often finding myself physically striking.

This often happens in the middle of a dream, and on one occasion I smacked Rinda in the gob with a vicious strike just as the swing tip went round, resulting in a retaliatory slap considerably below the gob line.

Rinda sometimes stares at me as if I have become possessed by some evil spirit, a surfeit of Tiger beer usually being responsible.

The Thais have no such problem with any form of memory loss or recollection and were a Thai brain to be dropped into a can of baked beans, its size and shape would render it indistinguishable from the rest of the contents.

* * * * *

This was never the case with the Singaporean natives.

I think that it is fair to say that my three years in Singapore protecting the Empire from all forms of communist aggression were deeply implanted in my memory banks, and were the inspiration, if not the major influence in my building the 18-lake fishery at Wolvey, a sleepy little village situated almost exactly halfway between Coventry and Leicester.

* * * * *

On my first Singapore day's match fishing with the fishing club of the Neanderthal Scottish battalion that I had unfortunately been attached to, I sat in wonder at the beautiful man-made pool, as common carp, golden carp, and good-sized cichlids cruised around looking for food.

Within an instant, the concept of a commercial fishery began to unfold.

The weight of fish contained in any given volume of water was directly related to both the oxygen and the food supply.

This I was to discover many years later as I set up the fishery.

If you overstocked a lake, the fish would be permanently hungry and much easier to catch, the caveat of course, is that if the anglers did not throw in enough food, the fishery owner would have to make up the shortfall.

Things began to fit into place weekly as I fished every one of the matches available on Singapore Island. The lakes that were the most heavily stocked were naturally enough the most popular, but if the fish were to be constantly caught, they needed to be quite robust and fast-growing, the latter meaning that they would forever be on the lookout for food and always hungry.

A constant companion for many of my fishing days was an American girl called Sue, who after a few tentative attempts at reducing the frequency of my fishing trips, eventually gave up and took up fishing herself.

God's benevolence one day came in the form of a transfer from the Scottish Regiment to an outfit a little more civilized and one that had mastered the English language.

I was now posted to Sembawang and put in charge of the Cashier's Department.

The fox was in the hen cote.

* * * * *

Flip, Boz, Col, Wayne, and I were sat in Sembawang barracks, our eyes glued to a 12-inch black and white TV.

It was Saturday night, and before heading into town in search of fresh female company in the floozy rich meat market known as Boogie street, we never missed an episode of Kung Fu, starring David Carradine.

CAN ANYONE REMEMBER DAVID CARRADINE IN KUNG FU?

Just as Grasshopper was about to fight a Chinese assassin who had travelled to America to kill him, the phone outside the barrack room door rang.

Being the senior rank, I cursed, walked outside, and picked up the phone intending to tell whoever was on the opposite end to sod off until the fight was ended.

"Is that the Naval Barracks?" came the rather gruff Lancastrian voice.

"NO." I almost shouted. "The poofs are in the next block; we are the army."

"No problem," the voice went on. "My name is Mick Miller, and I would like to invite a few of you lads over for a party at my place. There are half a dozen young girls who will look after you and as much booze as you can drink."

"Wonderful idea." I said, "Now sod off."

I put the phone down and walked back into the barrack-room, just as Grasshopper was halfway through his battle with the assassin. The last thing I needed at this critical point in time was some idiot winding me up.

Half a dozen young girls and free booze indeed - what a nincompoop coming up with such a stupid wind up.

Grasshopper was in trouble - the phone rang again - damn.

I dashed outside the room.

"Yes?" I shouted.

"Please don't put the phone down." The voice began to sound genuine. "This is not a joke. Many years ago I was in the Royals and was stationed at Sembawang barracks myself. The party is real, the girls are real, and the free booze is real. What's you name by the way?"

"Billy."

"Just a second then Billy." There were a few seconds silence before he spoke again. "Sue, come over and speak to Billy, he's in the army."

My knees went weak at the sexiest voice I have ever heard.

"Why don't you come over Billy and bring a few friends with you. We have some great country music and lots of drink. There are 6 of us, so bring a few good-looking guys along."

I dashed in the barrack-room - Grasshopper had just killed the assassin - grabbed a pen and paper and copied out the address as Sue spelt it out.

One hour later, the taxi pulled up outside a rather luxurious house in the upmarket Toa Paio district, and 4 showered, sweet-smelling squaddies climbed out and knocked on the door.

Poor Wayne was on duty and had to spend the night in the guard room looking after a couple of the previous night's drunks.

The door opened and this gorgeous blond American girl around 17 years old stood in front of us.

Four mouths and four sets of eyes opened wide.

"Hi, I'm Sue, which one of you guys is Billy?"

Four voices answered in unison.

"I'm Billy." They all said.

"No, you're bloody well not." I almost shouted. "I'm Billy."

Little did I know that Sue was about to become my fishing consort for much of my stay in Singapore.

The 4 of us followed the gorgeous Sue into this fabulous house, and sure enough, 5 other girls were inside dancing to country music.

A chap walked up and as he shook all our hands, introduced himself as Mick Miller.

"We're off now, so look after the girls," he cheerfully said, and with that, 4 adult couples walked out of the house, hand in hand, and climbed into a sort of minibus. "Be back around one, have fun." He said as he climbed in.

In the corner of the room was a bar stacked with enough booze to fill an Olympic sized swimming pool, so we tucked into both the Bacardi and the girls.

At spot on one o clock in the morning, the minibus turned up, and out climbed 4 drunken couples, noticeably holding on to a different partner to the one that they had left with.

"Jump in the taxi lads, I've already paid the driver, and he will take you back to the barracks. See you same time next week." Mick said before going inside.

Sure enough, after watching Kung Fu, we jumped into a taxi the next week and the process was repeated, the adults noticeably pairing up with different women. We had in fact stumbled into a wife swapping group, and as the girls were fully aware of this, they were given enough rope to hang themselves many times over - enough said.

This carried on for several weeks, until one night, just as we were ready to return to barracks, Mick told us to come at 2 in the afternoon the next Saturday as he had arranged a 25th-anniversary party for his wife Vicky.

We did, and what a party it turned out to be.

The garden was full of Texas oil men, all of whom worked for Petronas, the Malayan national oil giant, and pretty damned drunk as we all were on the gallons of champagne on offer, we all listed intently as "The Miller told his tale."

On leaving the Royal Navy, Mick joined the Merchant Navy as ships engineer, and after a long voyage to Hong Kong, had to dock up for a couple of weeks due to a spot of local bother.

Eventually, the cargo was loaded, and the ship set sail for England, only to find themselves stuck in the Gulf for a couple of months as the Suez War broke out and the Suez Canal was closed.

As the conflict ended, the canal was blocked and so they now had to sail around Africa, eventually arriving in Southampton after almost 5 months at sea.

Mick collected his long-overdue wages in cash, stashed it in a shoe box and boarded a train for his Blackpool home.

After what had seemed like a never-ending journey, he eventually arrived at Blackpool, and on his way to the house couldn't resist calling into his local pub for a drink - and what a drink it turned into.

Mick's next recollection was waking up on the sofa, covered from head to toe in mud and soil and minus his shoe box that had contained some 7000 quid.

Bit by bit, he began to piece together the previous night's exploits, eventually remembering that he had buried the shoe box in the garden and was going to surprise Vicky with it in the morning.

It was then that he remembered that he didn't have a garden, so he had obviously buried it in someone else's garden and had no idea which one.

Taking a spade from his shed, still drunk, he then began to retrace his steps back to the pub, digging up every likely looking patch of garden in Blackpool before being arrested and thrown in Blackpool nick.

BURIED TREASURE

Word spread like wildfire about this mad man who was digging up flower beds looking for buried treasure; even the local papers got in on the act.

Eventually, Vicky bailed him out, and still covered from head to toe in muck and soil, she took him home.

Mick was determined to find his money, and a couple of days later was again locked up for digging up someone's daffodil border.

By now, as you can imagine, the entire party was legless with both laughter and champagne.

Mick ended the story by telling us how the magistrate had almost died laughing and let him off with a fiver fine - he never found his money.

It was perhaps an hour or so later that Vicky came over and replaced Sue on my knee.

"He didn't lose the money, Billy," she said. "I went to the pub to collect him and found him on his knees digging away at a flower border a couple of houses away and dug it up after he staggered home. I bought a nice house with it at Lytham and told him that Mum had given it to me.

Don't tell Mick now, or I'll tell him what you have been up to with our Susan - she tells me everything."

Blackmail???

No, not really, more a case of Mutually Assured Destruction, I guess.

CHAPTER 13

THE STICK FLOAT

"Don't even think about it," Rinda said as she read my thoughts.

The two old Japanese gentlemen leaning over the parapet of Thailand's Bridge over the River Kwai offered a tempting target and having just visited the war museum, I felt an overwhelming urge to push them over.

THE BRIDGE OVER THE RIVER KWAI

Perhaps they weren't old enough to have been there during the occupation, nevertheless, their dad's might have been ...... who knows?

I gazed down at Thailand's perfectly replicated River Trent

and momentarily climbed aboard my Tardis, mentally turning back my over-active time clock to my early schoolboy days.

I guess that I would be around 11 years old, and the Grand Master himself, Benny Ashurst and dad were involved in a titanic peg for peg duel on the Bridgewater canal at Leigh.

Dad was fishing a small piece of peacock quill under his rod tip and Benny had just cast his STICK FLOAT to the far bank.

SO..... what was Benny Ashurst doing fishing a stick float on a canal?

Around this time, casting reels were just beginning to appear, and the long-established orthodoxy of fishing well over depth under the rod tip was being challenged.

There were no wagglers in those days, so a float that could reach the far bank needed to be invented.

Now Leigh was slap bang in the middle of the cotton industry at the time, and Blake's dark satanic mills cast a permanent foreboding shadow on the canal, blocking out much of the sunlight; these mills also contained millions of the world's most perfectly shaped stick float stems, crafted in a wood that was virtually buoyancy neutral, this final fact being critical.

These stems were the spindles on which the cotton was wound, and all that was needed was for a spigot to be whittled and shaped on the thick end once the pulley section had been sawn off, and the correctly shaped balsa was then glued on.

The earlier stick floats consisted of cane and peacock quill, which for some reason never worked correctly, and someone, probably Benny, found that the balance achieved by correctly shaping the balsa worked perfectly.

The finished float was fastened top and bottom using bicycle valve rubber and a BB shot pinched on about a foot from the hook.

Benny was fishing up to 3 foot over depth and casting to the far bank, the line being tightened to the float, which then became half-cocked as it followed a direct line to the BB shot, something that could never be achieved with the cane/peacock combination.

This was the unintentional beauty of the stick float – it always pointed directly at the bait because of the neutral buoyancy of the stem.

Fished on a river, this phenomenon is even more noticeable and critical to success.

I have to point out that the early sticks were NOT made of lignum vitae, these floats always sat vertically in the water and did not point directly at the bait. Because of the stem weight, they were useful for fishing at a greater range.

Once correctly balanced and in line with the bait, bites were almost always quite unmissable, because the moment the fish moved the BB shot, the float lay flat.

A MOUTH-WATERING SELECTION OF STICK FLOATS

Because Leigh was the home of 4 of the country's top maggot breeders, the Leigh anglers were many years in front of the rest of the country in the development and use of casters and began to dominate the Northern canal circuit. Unchallenged victory after victory became the weekend norm until in exasperation, Wigan Centre put in a motion to ban the bait in all their matches, as the Leigh anglers continued to take the Wigan bloodworm anglers apart with their stick float and caster approach.

Sooner or later, the Trent had to appear on the Leigh angler's radar and being the only anglers on the banking with pints of sinking casters, winning would have been almost a foregone conclusion if only they could sort out the shotting of the stick float.

Naturally, a single BB shot fished well over depth did not work on a flowing river, and over time was replaced by multiple smaller shot strung down the line enabling the bait to rise and fall whenever a brake was applied to the float.

The float now began to behave as only a stick float can, always pointing directly at the bait.

With this fundamental change in shotting and line control, an important chapter in angling history was written.

Strange to think that the origins of what was, and still is, the most successful river float in history began life on the Leigh canal and owes its birth to the Lancashire cotton industry.

CHAPTER 14

DEANIE

I've moved on a good few year, perhaps around the late 70's, to a time when John Dean and I were once again locked in a head-to-head race for the Matchman of the Year competition, to a time when the great Trentmen team had total domination of the river.

THE GREATEST TRENT TEAM EVER ASSEMBLED

Ah ------ the name John Dean.

This was a bogey man – a name that kept grown matchmen trembling in a state of permanent fear and anxiety – a man who ate new-born babies for breakfast – a man who was seemingly unbeatable on his local River Trent.

The time was mid-winter and John now held all the aces in what was becoming an annual duel between us for the coveted title.

It was the coldest winter ever known and all of mankind prayed for global warming.

All still-waters had a near 12-inch ice lid on them, and the only matches being held were on the Trent. This was John Dean's home – this was the river he had been hatched in following a liaison between two of the river's roach.

At an early age, he had climbed out of the river and moved to Selston.

Week after week, no one could even get a bite, conditions were so bad.

John Dean could.

John Dean had relatives living in the river.

In reality John was a quiet unassuming guy who never realized just how good he was; I would have given my right arm for half his talent.

* * * * *

One day, I heard about a match being run by Del Root on the Grand Union canal and was informed that it was always free of ice. I believe it was called the Running Horses pound, somewhere North of London in Southern Woofter land. The River

Gade flowed in at one end and out again a couple of miles along keeping the ice at bay.

Mid-week, I received a phone call from an old mate of mine from my Northern days', a likeable rogue called Roy Meredith, who at the time scraped bloodworm for a living. Roy was one of the four likeable rogues calling themselves "The Firm", a name coined for them by a Wigan reporter called Jack Winstanley.

Roy was short of cash as no one in the North West could go fishing because of the ice and he had 60 packs of bloodworm going cheap.

I drove up from the midlands and met Roy at Keele service station on the M6, handed over 60 quid, and collected the 60 packs of bloodworm, plus a special one for myself, knowing that no-one at the weekend's match down South would have any and I would be able to make a few bob.

My travelling companions at the time were Bill Spragg and Mick cotton, and that very week, Bill had managed to procure a barrel of chrysoidine from a light-fingered mate who worked in a paper mill.

I bought the barrel from Bill for not a lot of money, and so it was that 60 packs of bloodworm to be sold at 3 quid each, and 60 packs of chrysoidine at 5 quid each, made their way down the M1 on the Sunday morning.

* * * * *

Incidentally, it was the same chrysoidine that turned half of the women in the office yellow after I had added a spoonful to the coffee jar. It was also the same chrysoidine that found its way into a mate's sock that was hanging on the washing line. As he undressed a few days later, he became convinced that he had gangrene and would have to have his leg amputated.

* * * * *

Despite the car heater being on full blast, the windows of the car continually froze over on the inside as we headed South, it was so cold, minus 12 - I kid you not.

Eventually, after much to-ing and fro-ing, we found the match headquarters.

On arrival, I set about my Del Boy routine, and within minutes all of the bloodworm and chrysoidine had disappeared, and a few hundred quid would be heading North up the M1 later that day.

This was turning into a good day, somehow, I had the feeling that John Dean's narrow lead in the Matchman of the Year race was about to be overturned.

The swim I drew was like any other in the match length, but the quality of angler surrounding me was pretty darn good.

The weather over the past few weeks had been so bad, that only mad dogs and serious fishermen had left the comfort of their beds.

On my left was Mick Hyatt, one of the best canal anglers in the country, and two pegs to my right was Johnny Warren, a little further along was Dickie Carr.

I looked at the canal.

This was a canal in name only. It was flowing left to right at a pace slightly slower than the Trent, so all thoughts of canal greys and bread punches were ditched.

This was stick float water of your dreams.

Even though the sun was shining, the temperature was still well below zero, and that meant one thing only. Rock hard fishing and bloodworm.

Here was the first problem - how to feed the bait in what was effectively a flowing river?

Somehow, I had to keep a constant flow of bloodworm moving through the swim as would be normal river practice, but loose feeding was out of the question as half a dozen worm thrown by hand would not go far enough.

I thought about this for some time until the penny finally dropped.

I mixed up a bowl of groundbait so dry that it would barely hold together and burst on impact with the water; the bloodworm would be released and the dry groundbait float off along the surface.

Problem number 2.

It was so cold that everyone's rod rings froze, and their floats sailed down the canal in short, sharp, jerky movements.

Solution? - Simplicity itself. A few drops of glycerine on the spool and the stick float did whatever you asked of it. How many people know this?

The fishing was dire, and the word on the grapevine was that only 2 fish had been caught by mid-day.

Mick and Johnny disappeared up't pub, as did a few more anglers and soon I was pleasure fishing.

Perhaps halfway into the match, the float sank, and I slipped the net under a half-pound roach.

"Look out John Dean, I am coming to get you," I said to myself.

The rest of the match was what true fishing was all about.

The fish wanted to feed but did not want to be caught.

For the anglers who regularly fish the stick float, you will know exactly what I mean by that statement.

No matter how often the stick sails down, only occasionally the planets align. There comes a point where suddenly, everything is just so perfect that a bite is guaranteed.

You can feel this point - it may only happen once every few

casts, but when it does, you know that at that one single point in time, even if it is for no more than a couple of seconds, you have magically reached perfection, and you and the fish have become one.

Why was John Dean so good?

Simple really, John recognised this sweet spot - John reached that fleeting moment of perfection more often than the rest of us did.

Practice only makes good - you need a God-given gift to make perfect.

Despite winning the match, I didn't get my 10 Matchman of the Year points that day, only 79 fished and the rules demanded 80.

If anyone reading this article was the absentee ……. you bounder.

Still, it had been a profitable day, only spoiled by the news that John flippin Dean had scored a near double on the Trent that same weekend.

JOHN DEAN – JUST ANOTHER DAY AT THE OFFICE

I knew that the game was up, and once again resigned myself to being the bridesmaid to the phenomenon known as John Dean.

GOTCHA DEANIE.

On a brighter note, I did finally manage to beat the great Deanie one year to the most prestigious title in matchfishing.

Even then he finished second, and naturally enough he annihilated me the next year.

CHAPTER 15

BLOODWORM

For as long as I can remember, Billy has always been my favourite name, I can't think why.

For those of you of a rather more mature vintage, perhaps you can remember when we used to call big perch Billys?

Have you ever wondered why?

I thought not, so I am going to tell you.

Following the relocation of Harry Settle's bread punch and canal float, I had received a smack round the ear from dad. Stealing carried the death penalty in a Lancashire coal mining community. "I was going to give them back", I pleaded. "I only borrowed them". That lead to another slap, lying was only slightly less serious.

Time moved on a couple of years and equipped with a set of punches and a collection of balsa floats, (perhaps early canal greys) I had just weighed in a little over 3lb of roach on the Runcorn arm of the Bridgewater canal at Norton. I was feeling quite pleased with myself as I had just pipped my great rival, Albert Bailey junior who had been sat a couple of pegs away.

Albert was the youngest member of the Bailey family, all

match fishermen and all called Albert. As you can imagine, this caused problems with the match organisers, so they were referred to as Albert Bailey Snr - the grandad, Albert Bailey - the dad, and Albert Bailey Jnr or young Albert - the son. As my dad's name was also Billy, he was called Billy Makin Snr and I became Billy Makin Jnr or young Billy.

Albert, the father was quite a decent angler, Albert the son was quite superb, a real class act, and despite being my biggest rival on the Northern circuit we were always the best of friends. This friendship was severely tested when he denied me the title of English schoolboy angling champion - the bounder.

As we walked down the canal together, we could see a crowd of anglers stood behind Albert the father. "What have you got dad?' Albert the son asked.

"I've got a net full of Billy Bostons", came the reply.

Albert Jnr and I looked at each other and shrugged our shoulders.

Now Billy Boston played for the Wigan rugby league team; I had watched him many times.

Billy Boston was big - Billy Boston was black - Billy Boston played in the hooped colours of Wigan - Billy Boston dispensed with the niceties of running around defenders on the rugby field, much preferring to simply trample underfoot everyone that got in his way.

BILLY BOSTON – GET OUT OF MY WAY

SAME DEFIANT LOOK

As the scales arrived, Albert Bailey, the dad, lifted out his keep-net, and everyone gasped. The net was full of whacking great perch, full of bruising great Billy Bostons; big, almost black, and wrapped in the hoops of Wigan.

Over the next few years, these near black perch became more and more prominent in all matches on the Bridgey, and with time the name was shortened to simply Billys ------ my favourite name.

*****

The story begins at Leigh Grammar school, where in our metalwork classes we were given a free hand and tasked with making something that would be useful around the house.

Half of the lads made pokers for the coal fires that everyone had in those days, and the other half made toasting forks. No one had electric toasters, and the sound of mums scraping the burned bits off the toast echoed each morning around every house throughout the Lancashire coalfields' as they readied us for school.

This awkward little rascal decided to make neither a poker nor a toasting fork, instead, I set about constructing a perfect, state of the art bloodworm scraper; this from scraps of information gleaned from a Wigan kid who was in our class.

Complimenting this engineering wonder was a magnificent handle that screwed onto the blade, this being made in the woodwork class.

Normally, neither subject interested me, so both teachers were quite impressed at finding me suddenly quite attentive.

*****

Now even though match attendances were in their hundreds at the time, angling equipment was extremely limited, most anglers using greenheart, Tonkin, or split cane rods coupled with centrepin reels. The more adventurous ones were experimenting with fixed spool reels even though the waggler float was still someway in the future, and the tubular steel Taper Flash and Taper Flex rods were just beginning to appear.

Fishing a combination of baits and techniques during the course of a match was relatively rare in those days owing to both tackle limitations and financial restrictions, and so 3 distinct camps developed.

Wigan angler fished exclusively with bloodworm - Leigh anglers fished exclusively with the recently discovered caster, and Bolton anglers (the limited few in the know), fished with the secretive bread punch, coupled with squatts and homebred pedigree specials and pinkies.

I have mentioned before that I was pretty much an obsessive, and refused to accept only one form of fishing, resolving to familiarise myself with what seemed to be the three different branches of the sport.

This is much easier when you are young as your mind is not closed, nor is it set in any one direction, and as most of the memory banks are still empty, useful information is soaked up like a sponge, more so if you live and breathe the sport. It goes without saying that much of my early thinking was based around the advice passed on every Friday evening over a cup of tea at Benny Ashurst's home.

*****

It was a Saturday morning as I climbed off the bus at the Wigan bus station equipped with my gleaming bloodworm scraper and screw-on handle, and headed off towards Central

Park, the home of Wigan rugby league club. I knew my way to the ground as dad and I had watched Leigh play Wigan on several occasions when I had stood in awe at the fearsome Billy Boston.

I didn't need to know the way; it was enough to simply follow my nose. The entire area stunk to high heaven on a warm still day, the source of the obnoxious perfume being the River Douglas which ran alongside the rugby ground.

The river was little more than an open sewer, unchanged since Victorian times, and carried along much of the human effluent flushed down the Wigan toilets, together with a toxic concoction of chemicals that were openly discharged untreated from the local factories.

I had noticed the smell on occasions when watching the rugby, wondering where on earth it came from, and as I approached the river, I understood.

I won't describe it any further as it isn't difficult to imagine an open sewer, but it looked like a very closely pegged match was already underway. Dozens of anglers lined the banks, scraping through the sewage collecting Joker, which was then deposited in a metal bowl and later washed out through a lady's nylon stocking, again in the sewage water.

**SOMETIMES A SOLID MESH NET IS
SCRAPED THROUGH THE OOZE**

I found a gap between the Wigan bloodworm scrapers as one man left for home and set to work sliding the blade through the stinking black ooze, each time coming up with what I guess would be several thousand tiny red jokers.

The river must have contained millions in every putrid yard of evil smelling ooze.

I stuck it for as long as I could before being physically sick, washed the joker in one of mum's nylon stockings, and set off for home, resolving to stick to the bread punch and caster in the future and to return mum's nylon stocking to her drawer when it had dried out.

I didn't go fishing the next day, nor did I go to school all the following week, nor the week after.

I was too ill to go to the doctors, and mum had to go to the clinic to bring the doctor to me, whereupon I was stuffed with all forms of anti-biotics.

The doctor told mum that the bacteria had entered my body through a small cut on my hand and I was lucky to be alive.

He was also amazed at what I had been up to; it seems that everyone knew about the River Douglas, and many pet dogs had died because of drinking its putrid, human effluent soup.

Forgive me if I seem to have a downer on bloodworm and joker, but when you have almost died as a result of collecting it, perhaps it is only natural to have a negative opinion.

As an afterthought, the funniest part of the whole saga came many years later when the NRA announced their plans to clean up the river.

Most of Wigan's bloodworm anglers were up in arms. They didn't want a river with "bloody fish" in it - they wanted an open sewer so that they could collect their joker; fishing with any other bait was unthinkable to the anglers from Wigan.

CHAPTER 16

BLOODWORM (2)

Purely as a point of historical interest, canal anglers of a certain vintage may be familiar with a group of Wigan anglers known as THE FIRM, one of whom, Roy Meredith, I have mentioned in a previous chapter, as he supplied my bloodworm for the Southern canal match that I have written about.

I was friends with all four of them, good lads, Roy, Frank Franklin, Bert Naylor, and their captain, Graham Joynt.

Graham was quite well off and provided the transport for the team utilizing either a big Volvo estate or occasionally his Mercedes, and so it was with some surprise when many years later he turned up for a match at Carr Mill Dam in a battered old Volvo that had definitely seen better days.

"Hard times Graham?" I said.

He burst out laughing as he spoke. "It's my Liverpool car, Billy. You don't think that I am stupid enough to park the Merc in Liverpool, do you?"

* * * * *

Their history of the Firm is perhaps a little chequered, particularly as to how they first came to prominence, and in many ways their exploits brought bloodworm fishing to the attention of much of the country, many anglers never having even heard of the bait.

The open match was at Rugeley, close to Cannock on the Trent and Mersey canal in the mid to late '60s, and as was normal in those days, the entry was well over 200. I was still frozen as we made the draw, having completed the 60-mile journey in Dad's Reliant Del Boy van, and as was usual, the heater wasn't working.

The match was fished under NFA rules and everyone in match fishing throughout the country, except for Wigan anglers who rarely fished with any other bait, knew that bloodworm was banned, in fact, possibly the only place in the entire country where it was allowed was on the Wigan Centre matches.

Dave Hanson of Bolton, a superb bread punch angler, should have won the match and I should have been second, however it didn't work out that way.

The 4 Wigan anglers all fished bloodworm and finished 1st, 3rd, 5th, and 6th, relegating Dave and myself to 2nd and 4th on the day.

As many anglers had seen them using the banned bloodworm, someone put in an objection which was soon backed up by several other anglers.

I can well remember the lovely old chap who was the organiser stating in front of everyone that the objections were overruled, as he had used bloodworms that he had collected from his garden muck heap that very morning, obviously knowing nothing of the bait and almost certainly having used brandlings.

It was a few days later that Jack Winstanley, a well-respected angling journalist and an Angling Times contributor, wrote about the incident in the Manchester Evening news. Himself coming from Wigan, and on this occasion jauntily wearing his patriotically leaning Wigan hat, Jack conveniently refused to let facts get in the way of his scripted version of events.

Facts often spoil a good story.

The article that he wrote told of the terrible jealousy of the better-known North and Midland match fishermen who had been thrashed on their own water by these 4 supermen from Wigan who he christened "THE FIRM", (that is how they got their name) completely ignoring the fact that Wigan anglers were the only match anglers in the country who knew nothing about any bloodworm bans.

I was always of the opinion that as the 4 lads were quite new to the open match scene, having only ever fished around the Wigan area and only ever fished bloodworm matches, they never even thought about bait bans. If they had wanted to cheat, they would not have had their bait in the open for everyone to see.

They not only had their bait open to the other anglers, but during the course of the match were quite innocently explaining how to both collect and use the bait to the anglers who were stood behind them.

As for the bloodworm and joker, I will explain a little more and question just how much it seriously impacted the country's match attendances.

You will be amazed at how dangerous the joker can be to the fish and how hazardous it is to the angler.

Don't let anyone tell you that it is a natural bait - it is not.

Fish never see a joker unless an angler feeds it to them; it is a completely different species to the bloodworm and lives in a totally different environment, one in which fish cannot survive.

*****

Quite a few years ago I was on the receiving end of some very inaccurate journalism by Angling Times. I was never quite sure whether this was a case of incompetence or a deliberate attempt to create a controversial situation out of what may well have been a very important issue.

The headlines read, "Billy Makin says bloodworm kills fish".

I never said anything so stupid, however, the right to reply to such an outrageous headline wasn't available and the resulting furore made me look rather silly.

Looking back on it, I can't blame the young chap who wrote the story, as like the majority of anglers and angling journalist in the country, both bloodworm and joker were something he had only heard about without actually seeing or using them, and like many people at the time, he probably thought that jokers were little more than immature bloodworm, which of course they are not.

I have explained why the collection of jokers can be so hazardous to health and having been made seriously ill on the only occasion that I attempted it, my match approach evolved into a different form of fishing the bait using only bloodworm, positively refusing to touch the potentially toxic joker.

* * * * *

The rather worrying story begins on the first match of one of Pat O'Connor's winter leagues held on the Oxford canal at Ivy Bridge. Perhaps I should first explain why Pat morphed into his alter ego of pedigree bloodworm entrepreneur and why the pseudonym took root.

On match day, Pat sold peat, all neatly packaged in polythene bags or wrapped in newspaper. Inside each bag would be a single, solitary, petrified bloodworm, invariably curled up into a little ball in an attempt to try and disguise itself as a lump of peat and so avoid being impaled on a size 24s hook.

Occasionally a whoop of delight was heard during a match, as some fortunate angler found a second bloodworm.

Pat got wind of this and tightened up his quality control.

On one occasion an angler almost fell in the canal when on opening his pack, he found 12 bloodworm - Pat had given him a team pack by mistake.

During the course of a season, most of the County Mayo peat bog crossed the Irish sea and was deposited weekly on the banks of the Oxford cut.

We all teased Pat mercilessly over his bloodworm packs, but to be honest, without them our weekend matches wouldn't have been quite the same.

ONE OF PAT'S REAL BLOODWORM PACKS

Now all of Pat's matches were a delight to fish, and our Oxford canal circuit was the envy of the country. Very rarely did an angler appear who wasn't on first name terms with every one of the 100 plus regulars, and it's fair to say that despite the rivalry and the often quite atrocious weather, every weekend was like a festive event, and every single angler became more and more excited with each passing day as the weekend approached.

I have to point out that this camaraderie did not extend to the rest of the Midlands' match circuit, where arguments, objections, and darn right bloody mindlessness destroyed several well-established Winter leagues.

While Pat supplied us all with a bloodworm each, a chap called George Longton (it may have been Longdon) came down from somewhere in the barren, frozen, northern wasteland known as Yorkshire with bucket loads of joker.

On this particular day, George was late, and we seemed destined to fish for a full 5 hours with our solitary bloodworm and nothing to feed with.

Eventually, he turned up little more than one hour before the match was due to start and supplied us with the evillest smelling joker imaginable, still in the filthy black sewage water from which he had collected it that very morning. Nevertheless, it was alive and kicking, so we hurriedly made our way to our swims, not having time to clean off the stinking mess that accompanied it.

It is only fair to point out that George's joker, like Pat's bloodworm, was usually in pristine condition and thoroughly cleaned off. I can't remember what went wrong on this occasion but it most certainly was a one-off.

**USUALLY BOTH PAT AND GEORGE'S BAIT
WAS IN PRISTINE CONDITION**

Ivy Bridge was pretty much a one method, one species venue, probably unique in the whole of the country in that the match-winning fish was the humble Tommy Ruffe, and for those who have never targeted the species, you will catch 10 on the bloodworm for every one that you catch on a pinkie.

At the end of the match I had around 5 pounds of the little blighters together with an odd small roach and perch and was a little concerned that when returning the fish after weighing,

I noticed that several of them sank to the bottom and appeared to be dead.

On returning home, I took the remaining joker into the living room and fed them to my fish in my large aquarium, something I had been doing for at least a couple of years.

The next morning, I was horrified to find that every single fish was dead - roach, perch, gudgeon, and ruffe. Most of the fish I had kept for several years, so only one thing could have killed them. What was also noticeable was that they were all dead on the bottom, none of them was at the surface.

Over the next few days, I made a series of phone calls to an old university friend of mine who was taking his biology masters and was surprised to discover that Jokers could not only survive in high levels of toxicity but could also feed and absorb these toxins into their bodies.

Once transferred to clean water, however, these toxins are purged, which would explain why water where jokers are cleaned up always turns filthy and stinks to high heaven.

These toxins can then be transferred to the fish once the uncleaned and unpurged joker has been eaten.

As a parallel, DDT killed the flies which in turn killed the birds that ate them and was soon subject to a worldwide ban.

The burning question of course is whether bloodworm and joker should be banned. Sure they help to catch fish when the going is tough, but at what cost to both the fish and many match anglers who either cannot afford them or cannot regularly obtain them?

I can pretty much guarantee that attendances dropped, as during the harsh winter conditions when bloodworm and joker fishing really comes into its own, they are usually the most difficult times to obtain them, and what about the quality of the fishing?

What about the complete preoccupation of the fish with bloodworm at the expense of all other baits?

I believe that this issue is pretty important if real fishing were to ever return, and at the moment this appears to be happening; it is even more important for anyone who owns or manages a fishery. I banned them from the outset on my lakes.

As an interesting after thought, it is illegal to bring fish into the country without rigorous health checks and certification, however, there appears to be no problem bringing in the contents of the European and Eastern Block sewage systems - that is where many of the joker sold in the country comes from.

Maybe that was the origin of many of our fish diseases - just a thought.

CHAPTER 17

BOB

"What the ecky thump are you up to Bob?" I asked one of the world's greatest anglers, as he carefully threaded a length of wire through each section of his pole before piecing it together.

Bob Nudd grinned.

BOB – ENOUGH SAID

He had rung me a couple of days earlier and was now sat on Lagoon pool on phase 2 of my lakes at Wolvey accompanied by a chap who was fiddling with a computer monitor.

Once fully assembled, I guess at around 9 or 10 meters, Bob

pushed out his pole into the lake, hanging from the end of it being around a foot of wire attached to a small black object perhaps the size of a matchbox.

I checked the monitor, and as I suspected the whole set up was a sonar device, enabling Bob to see everything that was happening in his swim.

Each individual fish sent back a signal and we could also follow the progress of a ball of groundbait as it sunk and disintegrate on its way down.

Bob took a walk with his pole, dropping the "matchbox" into different swims, the boffin fellow carrying the monitor.

"Billy," Bob shouted, as I talked to a fellow angler some 30 yards away. "Come and look at this."

He was now in a narrow section of the lake.

I walked over and could barely believe what the monitor was telling us.

The swim was about 6 feet deep, and at almost mid-depth was a solid bank of fish that stretched for some 5 yards in either direction containing hundreds of fish of all sizes.

Bob threw in a ball of groundbait.

The wall parted, and a couple of fish followed it down for a foot or so before returning to the main body of fish.

None of the other fish showed the slightest interest in the feed as soon as it had passed below them.

We were witnessing water stratification, a phenomenon anyone who has ever swum in a lake in hot, wind-free conditions will be familiar with.

The surface of the water can be almost bath water warm and remain so for perhaps 2 or 3 feet down, but it does not cool gradually by degrees. It sits in layers, with a dramatic temperature drop as your lower body encounters the lower layer.

The fish that Bob was now observing were all clumped together in the layer that was the most comfortable for them, and no amount of feeding would get them to leave their comfort zone.

Think of the implications of drawing such a swim - you could easily spend the entire match fishing below the fish and swear that the swim was barren.

I once drew such a swim at Attenborough Gravels; however, this swim was anything but barren. Basking just below the surface were hundreds of big, black, beautiful bream, and muggins here spent 5 hours trying to get them to go down into 14 feet of water, being equipped with only a quiver tip rod and no floats.

The following Wednesday, Bob Stevens of Long Eaton wasn't quite so stupid and caught 127lb in the same swim by fishing 18 inches deep.

Stratification is of course broken down by water movement, particularly strong wind.

In Summer, you want to be at the end of the lake where the wind blows into your face. The warm upper layer moves in your direction and folds under, meaning that the entire area consists of warm water.

The opposite effect will be felt by the poor blighters at the other end of the lake because all the warm water is pushed into the windward end, the colder lower layers moving to the other side of the lake.

On a cold Winter's day, however, everything is in reverse.

The cold surface water is not to the fish's liking.

They want to be in the warmer lower layer, this of course being the side of the lake where the wind is on your back.

Fish are really quite simple creatures, and no amount of exotic seat boxes will ever make up for a thinking angler's logic.

* * * * *

Not knowing the basics of water stratification, the England International team manager once almost destroyed the confidence of 2 of England's brightest young angling talents.

It was something that I was vaguely familiar with having covered the subject during A level classes at school, and something that I was reminded of during a match at Coombe Abbey lake one Summer's evening.

I had drawn well, way down in the low numbers, and was sat next to perhaps the greatest matchman of them all.

Ivan Marks left his peg some 15 minutes before the "all in" and came and sat behind me.

"You've upset Stan you know Billy," he said. "What's wrong with you, why don't you want to fish for England?"

I went cold.

Stan Smith, the England team manager had rung me a few weeks earlier asking me to join the team to fish the world championships.

It was a call I had been dreading and had long before decided that my answer would be no; Stan had promised to keep everything away from the press, and I, in turn, hadn't even told my best friends, so how come Ivan knew?

I explained to Ivan that I wasn't a team angler and would probably let the team down.

Ivan wasn't convinced and kept probing, so I opened up.

A few years earlier, the England team had had a disastrous world championship due to a rigid team plan that each team member had to stick to.

Ivan burst out laughing.

"I was there Billy," he said. "What a complete cock-up that was."

He then filled in the gaps that I was missing from the press reports of the match.

The venue was a large, deep, slow-moving canal, and during the practice sessions, the team had worked out that a sliding float fished around 14 feet deep down the middle was the killer method.

So effective was the plan, and so out of reach of the other teams who were all pole anglers, that it was a case of simply turning up and collecting the medals.

On the day of the match conditions had changed dramatically.

The canal was not moving, the wind had dropped completely, and the temperatures were equatorial.

The perfect storm for water stratification and so it turned out.

The team, containing 2 of the country's finest young angling talents, Tommy Pickering, and Mark Downes, were forced to spend the entire match staring at motionless floats as the continentals fished the upper layer for small fish.

TOMMY – WORLD CHAMPION – HEWN FROM ENGLISH OAK

Every time Stan Smith walked off, Ivan flicked out a small float on his whip and caught a fish a chuck.

Stan caught him once and told him to get back onto the slider and follow the team plan.

The team finished last, and I believe that Ivan and Tommy were the only ones to catch.

I can remember Paul Downes telling me that his brother, Mark, who had blanked, was devastated – fortunately, both young men were built of English Oak and developed into two of the country's top anglers, Tommy becoming a world champion and Mark becoming the England team manager.

ENGLAND TEAM SUCCESS FOR MARK DOWNES

Not only does stratification layer the water at different temperatures, in many cases the bottom layer is also subject to de-oxygenation, so it is quite probable that the entire team's hookbait was bobbing around in water strata that would have suffocated the fish.

Ask any River Severn angler what happens to the fishing when there is a release of cold, de-oxygenated water from the Clywedog dam.

Ivan understood why I had made my decision even though he did not agree with it.

He had almost lost his England team place as a result of not sticking to a rigid team plan.

YOU DO NOT TELL IVAN MARKS, ONE OF THE WORLD'S GREATEST ANGLERS HOW HE HAS TO FISH.

Incidentally, one of us won the Coombe match with 8 bream and the other one came second with 7.

I won't tell you which one of us it was, but I resolved to get even with Mr Marks the next time we drew next to each other.

CHAPTER 18

SOMETHING TO THINK ABOUT

I am now going to break with my usual format and do something completely different.

I am going to go through some of my experiences in fishing, together with my observations on thought-provoking articles about fishing to make you think more about your fishing rather than simply following the accepted trends and fashions that most anglers seem to adopt nowadays.

First up is the question of exactly what the fish can see and how they react to an angler's presence.

* * * * *

Question one - Can the fish see what goes on directly above them?

Some years ago I was in Florence, Italy, at an international angling show standing on the Ponte Vecchio bridge over the River Arno, mesmerised by the actions of a shoal of chub directly below the bridge. People were dropping small pieces of bread which were being blown in all directions by a wind swirling around the bridge arches, and wherever the bread flew, the whole shoal followed, until on hitting the water, the nearest chub grabbed it and the entire shoal returned to the bridge.

THE BEAUTIFUL PONTE VECCHIO BRIDGE IN FLORENCE

So the answer is yes, they see everything above them, which poses questions as to the colour of the top sections of a pole and the colour of the float attached.

Maybe this is the reason why my canal floats were grey to blend in with the sky rather than the traditional black.

Interestingly, the colourless, see-through plastic floats used by many anglers are the most visible of all floats on a sunny day, the rays being passed down the float and appearing as a silver light at the base, pretty much similar to the tiny silver bubbles that flash on the feathers of a mackerel fly. I confirmed this for myself one day in an open-air swimming pool.

Whether or not this is a bad thing I don't know, as, in tropical waters, commercial fishermen shine bright lights directly into the sea at night in order to attract the shoal fish.

* * * * *

Question 2 - How do fish see anglers in highly coloured water?

We all know that this happens, and to present a skyline silhouette can be the kiss of death.

When I was a kid, I was an avid reader of the Angling Times and my favourite columnist was the late great Dick Walker, often referred to as the father of angling. I well remember one particular tale that was to come back and revisit me years later.

DICK WALKER WITH CLARISSA, HIS BRITISH RECORD CARP

Dick was fishing with a friend on I believe the River Ouse, catching a fish every swim down, his friend unable to catch anything. Being the chivalrous sort of chap that he was, Dick swapped swims, both anglers now using each other's tackle.

Soon Dick was again catching every swim down while his friend remained virtually bite less.

As his friend was a pipe smoker, Dick quite reasonably assumed that the tobacco tainting his friend's fingers stopped the fish from taking the bait.

Dick was right to point the finger of suspicion at the tobacco, but I believe that he came to the wrong conclusion.

It would be around 25 years later as I was sat on the second peg below Kings' Sutton lock on the delightful Oxford canal catching a gudgeon almost every cast, when Johnny Warren from Hinckley came and sat behind me, keeping well down in front of a hedgerow and well away from the skyline.

Perhaps 10 minutes after Johnny had sat down, the bites stopped completely, returning some 5 minutes later. This happened 4 times over the period that he sat behind me, each time coinciding with him striking a match to light his cigarette, each action producing a sudden explosive burst of infra-red.

I told Ray Mills, my travelling companion at the time as I drove home, and the very next week, he confirmed that exactly the same thing happened to him at Rickmansworth on the Grand Union; he had been fishing the far side of the canal, not close to his rod tip as I had been.

So looking back on Dick Walkers' story, his friend being a pipe smoker would have been striking his Swan Vestas every few minutes, providing innumerable flashes of infra-red and startling the fish every time.

Maybe the fish see in the infra-red, which would explain how the blighters can see people standing behind us despite highly coloured water.

Therefore, is it sensible to present a glowing infra-red image by not wearing a shirt in summer?

*****

Question 3 - Can fish see colour?

I am going to go back once again to an old article by Dick Walker. Now Dick had an aquarium in his home that was beside the front window, and at near enough the same time every morning, the red-breasted stickleback in the aquarium seemed to have a fit. This went on for weeks and puzzled him greatly, until one morning, he noticed the bright red post office van pull up outside of his window, the stickleback once again went berserk.

Dick observed this with much amusement and noticed that it only occurred when the red post van pulled up, not any other colour of vehicle.

He tried placing different objects in with the stickleback and found that they would attack anything, any shape or size, as long as it was red.

Here is a little confession to all you Black Country matchmen that Ray and I fished against on your stickleback infested canals.

We always took a couple of sticks with the bottom halves painted bright red. When the "Backs" became a nuisance, we agitated the sticks in the canal and the whole flippin lot of them finished up by our feet instead of in our swims.

Sorry chaps, didn't I mention that when we fished against you? Must have slipped my mind.

* * * * *

Question 4 - Can fish smell?

I'm not so sure that smell is the right word, perhaps taste would fit better.

I don't think that anyone who has ever shark fished in Florida would deny that a chum bag of chopped fish attracts them from miles away, so sharks certainly can smell.

Let me go back once again to Dick Walker and yet another of his thought-provoking articles.

In his aquarium along with the stickleback he had a couple of small perch, and like most anglers, he was always on the look-out for a fish-attracting scent.

One day as an experiment, he dropped a lobworm into a bucket of water, left it for a few minutes, stirred the water, and then took one single drop from the bucket and dropped it into his aquarium.

The reaction was instant, both of the perch immediately picking up the scent and dashing around looking for the source of what to them was hidden food.

The quantity of worm juice, for want of a better description, couldn't have been more than a few parts per million, nevertheless, Dick had now discovered what he wanted to know.

Yes, fish can detect a smell, and yes, certain smells excite the fish into feeding mode.

Here now is where it all becomes rather complicated.

Which smell works and which smell does the fish recognize as a possible pollutant and shy away from?

Is there any consistency in the attractive properties of additives when climatic and temperature changes are factored in? Certainly, different bait preferences are noticeable when conditions change.

I am talking about groundbait, so here is a little true story that greatly influenced my match fishing for most of the time that I was active on the Midlands' circuit.

When I moved into Sandy Crescent in Hinckley during the late 70's, I decided to dig a garden pond and stock it with gudgeon and roach. Fortunately, after 2 days of digging, much effort, and little to show, Mick Cotton turned up one weekend and set to work after I promised him a season ticket for the pond. Things moved on quickly from there, and I helped by keeping Mick supplied with food and drink without actually having to break into a sweat.

Now the pond was only about 8 foot long and little more than a couple of feet deep yet proved more than popular with Ray Mills during the 3-month closed season, in fact, some mornings I would wake up, look through my bedroom window, and see this overgrown garden Gnome already at work among the gudgeon.

MY CLOSED SEASON ESCAPE

I set up 2 six-foot whips with identical terminal tackle and then began a series of experiments over several weeks until the fishing season again opened. I fished one side of the pond feeding only bread crumb, and Ray swapped and changed between a variety of the new flavoured groundbaits that were just beginning to appear, his bait being some 6 feet away from mine.

Never once - not on one single occasion did the plain bread crumb fail to produce the most fish.

We then tried every spice and flavouring known to man, and still, the bread crumb always won hands down whichever side of the pond it was used on.

Some of the concoctions and spices lead to the entire stock of fish moving to the other side of the pond, resulting in a complete blank on the pole swim fed with the additive. I can only assume that the fish recognised the additive as some form of pollutant or irritant.

I, like every other match angler, would have loved to have found the magic formula for groundbait and bait, but were we simply chasing rainbows and losing sight of the fact that correctly timed introductions of groundbait in the right quantities were far more likely to influence our catches than some witches brew concocted in a Chemistry lab.

* * * * *

I am now going to tell a story that completely contradicts what you have just read, but in many ways ties in with the Dick Walker lobworm story.

One year, most of the roach throughout the country disappeared during the closed season, succumbing to a disease known as columnaris. This would be around the time that I had just had my run with the newly developed swing tip at Carr Mill Dam.

Nature abhors a vacuum, and soon the Warrington AA stretch

of the Bridgewater canal saw a perch explosion so big that there was little point fishing for any other species - to catch one single roach during the next 2 or 3 years was a talked-about event.

One Friday, dad and I picked up our usual supply of maggots from Benny Ashurst's house and found that they were straight off the maggot bed, still with the feed sack and smelling strongly of ammonia. To keep them from sweating up I tipped a couple of pounds of dry brown crumb in with them.

And so it was that later that week, Dad, Norman Hewitt and I were sat during the afternoon at Grappenhall on the Bridgewater cut having a practice chuck before the evening's match a couple of miles up the canal.

Not wishing to waste 2lb of perfectly good groundbait, I used the riddled, smelly stuff that the maggots had been cleaned up in, and we were all soon in action.

After some 30 minutes, Norman's swim, 20 yards to my left, and downstream in the slightly flowing canal dried up, and 5 minutes later so did dad's swim between Norman and myself. Mine however burst into life, so much so that both dad and Norman stood open-mouthed behind me as half-pound perch grabbed the bait within seconds of it hitting the water; I swear that I have never caught fish so quick even in Ireland.

The only logical conclusion had to be that every perch in both Norman and dad's swim had moved up the canal to the source of the scent.

Using the smelly groundbait, I won the evening match by a

country mile, and the following Monday, Benny's afternoon match on the Runcorn arm, and the same evening, the Runcorn AA match, every single fish being a perch.

I never quite recaptured the magic of that one batch of groundbait, but I have to say that I did pretty well over the next few years until the roach recovered and again began to dominate; a new disease which the press called perchitis decimating the perch stocks.

* * * * *

While still on the subject of groundbait, during the latter part of my match fishing days I found myself up against the "Balling" brigade on the canals.

I never had trouble balling it in myself but certainly never on canals; it was usually at 50 yards range when bream fishing on the lakes or even bream rivers, but to find a nincompoop balling 6 Jaffa's filled with joker into a boat busy canal on the next peg was the kiss of death.

THE KISS OF DEATH

Six balls of joker would contain tens of thousands of the creatures, and the first canal barge to pass will scatter them and the fish all over the place.

* * * * *

Question 5 - So, did balling it in work other than when trying to hold a bream shoal?

Back to the large aquarium in my home at Sandy crescent in the days before I poisoned all the fish with the contaminated joker.

Occasionally, I would drop maybe 20 or 30 pinkies into the tank in one go.

Rarely would the fish become too excited once the pinkies had reached the bottom, so as ever, I just had to experiment.

I would drop the 20 pinkies into one side of the tank, and every few seconds drop a single pinkie into the other side.

Within very little time, every single fish of all the species were competing for the falling pinkies and completely ignoring the free meal waiting for them on the other side of the tank.

I have to say that this observation influenced my whole approach to fishing for the rest of the time that I competed in matches.

Shoal fish are programmed to compete and not graze, that was the reason why I never subscribed to any form of "Balling" it in on a canal. Once in you cannot take it out; you can however adjust the frequency and amounts of feed on a little and often basis as determined by the response of the fish.

As a final comment on the balling it in issue: - have you ever seen a more boring spectacle masquerading as a sport than the freshwater fishing world championships?

God know how many anglers spending 5 minutes throwing up to 20 near coconut sized balls into the water in front of them and then spending the entire match holding a great chunk of carbon fibre in the hope that their twenty balls will somehow be better than everyone else's twenty balls.

Fishing used to involve watercraft, subtlety, finesse, innovation, and inspiration, not the mindless boredom dished up by the world championships.

It is no wonder that the media shows little interest in the sport.

CHAPTER 19

WHERE DID OUR HISTORY GO?

During mid-summer I occasionally sit in front of the TV watching the final stages of the British Golf Open, usually with a great deal of envy; not because of the money or the fame on offer - no, it's something far more important than that, or at least is for me.

I envy the fact that the result of every British Open ever held is not only recorded for posterity, but every winner, seemingly since before time began, has retained his special place in golfing history.

This retention and emphasis on history applies to all 4 of the Golf Majors.

The commentators go on about what Tony Jacklin had for breakfast on the final day of his Open winning debut all those years ago, while the majority of today's anglers would probably be pushed to even name any of England's former world angling champions', and there has been a heck of a lot of them, Alan Scotthorne having won it 5 times and Bob Nudd 4 times.

Everyone in golf knows that Harry Vardon won the Open 6 times and can probably tell you what he also had for breakfast on every last day.

The great Billy Lane became England's first world angling champion, yet how many anglers can even name a national angling champion let alone how many eggs he ate for breakfast that morning.

MAYBE THE GREATEST MATCH ANGLER EVER

Despite being a tiny minority sport when I was a lad, and a sport with extremely limited access for 90% of the population, golf has both developed and retained its' own history.

Golf lives on its' history and a good deal of its' folklore.

Angling has forgotten its history; in fact, we don't have one despite for many years being the country's biggest participant sport by a country mile.

Who can tell me where casters were first developed, the bread punch, the first stick floats, when and where wagglers and sliders were first made and used?

OK, so you have just read it, but did you know beforehand?

The early pioneers are almost certainly long gone now, but why have we let their memory go with them?

I know a little of the men and methods of the beginning of the Golden Age of Match Fishing, maybe you now also know a little and have an insight as to how many items of modern-day tackle evolved.

It would perhaps be a little churlish to claim that pole fishing originated on the continent and was brought over to Britain by the English world fishing team - Londoners had been using what they called the roach pole long before any of the English team had even been born.

Many of the stories relating to the Golden Age began in the Lancashire coal mining and cotton mill town of Leigh in Lancashire close to where I grew up, and where I occasionally went to school between fishing days.

Dad was quite a good match angler, but in his late teenage years, not only was tackle primitive but money and resources were in short supply.

These were austere early war and post-war years.

Yes, all you younger anglers out there, Britain was a little more than slightly involved in the second world war.

Groundbait and maggots were luxuries, and as I have pointed out in previous chapters, were usually replace by finely sieved black dirt and chopped worms, coupled with whatever maggots could be homebred.

Nothing was wasted in those days, and burnt toast and stale bread were always saved, much of it collected from neighbours, to be ground down into a rough type of groundbait in a metal mince beef grinder that you screwed and locked onto the side of the kitchen table. This gave another bait option of pinched bread on the hook, that is if you managed to smuggle a couple of slices out of the kitchen when mum was off her guard.

During my early adolescence, I received many a rocket for climbing onto neighbours' coal sheds to collect the stale bread that they had put out for the birds and an even bigger rocket for shooting the pigeons that came down to feed on it.

I wasn't aware of it at the time, but the maggots that I bred from the pigeons were in fact gozzers, they simply supplemented my bait for the weekend.

As a young man, dad's greatest rival was Benny Ashurst, father of Kevin, and in the early years, dad successfully competed against Benny, often more than holding his own.

This was to change, as Benny, together with 3 other local men, recognized the enormous hole in the market for maggots, and 5 of the country's 6 major maggot breeders began to emerge, 4 based around Leigh, the 5th one perhaps some 20 miles away, with number 6 close to Sheffield.

As previously mentioned, the country's only 2 squatt breeders set up, again around Leigh, both men's sons attending the same school as I did and being friends.

I now have to enter a little into the realms of folklore, as the emergence of the caster and its early use has been claimed by many people, however, I am pretty sure that the following historical account is correct as it was personally recounted to me by Alf Pendelbury himself.

Alf was sat on the banks of the River Severn during a summer heatwave competing in a big match, probably somewhere in the 1950's. Now as Alf was one of the big 4 Leigh maggot breeders, (I worked for him during the school holidays some years later) he had a big container of maggots, which was quite a rarity in those days as the average angler could barely afford more than a handful for the hook and feeding with them was almost unheard of.

With the heat, his maggots began to turn, and he noticed a few fish topping in his swim every time that he fed, so as an experiment he slipped a caster on his hook.

Immediately, he was into a big roach.

Next cast - the same result, and so it continued.

Who should come walking down the banking?

You can probably guess.

Benny Ashurst was more than a little interested and sat behind Alf for some considerable time and being one of the big 4 Leigh maggot breeders himself, he immediately set to work on how to stop the casters from floating, discovering that if riddled soon enough and dropped into water they would remain sinkers, and if the water was constantly changed they could be kept usable for days.

BENNY ON HIS WAY TO NEAR IMMORTALITY

Leigh became the birthplace and the home of the caster, and with it began to produce some of the finest anglers in the country.

Throughout the rest of the country, anglers had to rely on the tackle shops for their maggots - Leigh anglers simply popped along to the nearest of the 4 maggot breeding farms and collected pints of bait for a fraction of the cost.

Firstly though, owing to the primitive tackle on offer, ways had to be developed to capitalize on the fact that wherever they went, the Leigh anglers would be the only ones with quantities of the deadliest bait yet discovered.

It must be remembered that the advent and impact of the caster were more of an evolutionary process rather than a revolutionary one, so the chronology is difficult to recall as records are not available.

As I said, angling has lost most of its' history, much of it being confined to folklore - a bit like religion really only much more important.

I would guess that the next great discovery, and dare I say revolution in bait development has to be the pellet, its' prominence being fueled by the commercial fisheries boom.

I cannot recall anyone using pellets when I first began work on Makin Fisheries, but I do remember buying a ton of pellets from BOCM Pauls in Bristol to feed the thousands of near fingerling carp that I first stocked my fishery with.

AN ARIEL VIEW OF MY 18 LAKE FISHERY

MAKIN FISHERIES – OPEN NOW AS A HOLIDAY COMPLEX

The company was producing the high protein pellets for the many businesses that were rearing rainbow trout for the table, and as larger carp were quite an exotic species at the time, the option of buying catchable fish simply did not exist.

Once feeding and fishing the pellet became commonplace a few years later, I recognized the problems that this caused.

The pellets were too high in fats and proteins, having been produced for carnivores (trout) and not omnivores, and were causing considerable liver damage to the carp. A reduction in fats and proteins was necessary, plus, and this is a very big plus, the darned fish began to grow at an alarming rate.

I banned all forms of pellet.

Did I do right?

I think so, the fish stopped growing and the biomass of the carp began to reach a balance with the food supply. Matchmen could now concentrate on catching reasonable sized fish without double-figure monstrosities figuring in catches.

On selling the fishery, pellets were reintroduced by the new owner, and from what I have been told, the weights went up but the quality of fishing went down, as stronger poles, lines, and elastics became the norm.

There are now far too many double figure carp in most commercial fisheries, and the tackle has to be tailored accordingly - maybe this is what has led to the upsurge in silverfish matches.

The novelty of multiple ton-up match weights has worn off, taking with it much of match fishing's magic.

A 400lb match-winning weight is an affront to the sport.

*****

In a previous article, I expressed skepticism at the impact of flavours being added to both bait and groundbait, however, there is little doubt that the introduction of fish meal changed the landscape somewhat.

The question of course is whether the effect is more pronounced on the angler than it is on the fish?

An instilled confidence in a certain mix or flavouring is difficult to shake off.

I sat behind Andy Findlay one day down my lakes during a match, and he was bagging up using a version of the now popular flat-sided feeder that he invented and developed, as anglers around him struggled.

Andy's feeder was filled with nothing more exotic than a finely riddled brown crumb, whilst various cocktails of flavoured fishmeal surrounded him on virtually every other swim.

Now I am well aware that Andy would catch carp under a bathroom shower, but what of the anglers around him - were they so busy looking for the magical fish-attracting formula that they were overlooking the far more important aspects of the game?

Perhaps even more intriguing that day was the fact that Andy was tucking 2 dead red maggots into his feeder.

Who on earth stuck dead maggots on their hook? Well, Andy did, and now everyone follows the one-time unthinkable practice.

Perhaps I should expose a little deception that I perpetrated for many, many years, without even revealing the secret to my travelling companion Ray Mills.

I NEVER USED A LIVE PINKY WHEN TARGETTING GUDGEON.

A fresh, wriggling pinky will result in 2 out of every 3 bites being missed - a dead and burst pinky ensures that 9 out of 10 bites results in a gudgeon joining its' mates in the keepnet.

There, I've finally said it - it has been difficult keeping such a secret for so long, but I mistakenly blurted it out on one of my videos, fortunately, no one picked up on it and I retained the advantage for many years.

Going back to the caster, how many people are aware that the colour of the bait is on occasions critical to what finishes up in the keepnet?

If decent sized perch or skimmers weighing up to a pound and a half are the targets, the caster on the hook has to be in its' early stages, not quite white, more a very light shade of orange - neither of the 2 fish categories particularly like a dark caster. Big bream prefer a darker caster tipped with a squatt, whilst quality roach usually prefer a caster so dark that it will float. For this reason, the top canal anglers always dried out a few casters and left them out in the sun during a match, the floating caster slowing down the descent of the bait and leading to many more bites on the drop.

Perhaps this is because with age comes wisdom, the older, wiser roach being harder to fool.

Not unlike us really, unless of course Thai bar girls are involved, then age is invariably accompanied by illogical irrationality.

Guilty as charged your honour.

CHAPTER 20

MY BROOKSIE

The Mills and I were off to a match on the Thames at Wolvercote, when with a glint in his eye, and a rather supercilious expression on his smug face, he quite nonchalantly mentioned that he now owned the best two match rods in the country.

Drawing a few swims downstream from Ray, I just had to pop along and see what he was up to - he wasn't wrong.

I gasped as I picked up and waggled his spanking new 12-foot Bruce and Walker carbon fibre gem. It wasn't just a thing of exquisite beauty compared to the glass fibre rod that I had been using for the past few seasons, this leap forward was the angling equivalent of putting a man on the moon; it was in fact NASA that was responsible for much of the development in carbon fibre.

This was indeed a giant leap for angling mankind.

I had been through Tonkin, greenheart, and split cane wooden rods, avoided the tubular steel apollo rods, and for many years used fibre glass, this however was a completely different ball game.

I rang up Jim Bruce, one of the two partners at Bruce and Walker, and arranged to go round to the factory that same week. I knew Jim quite well as he had rung me on several occasions trying to get me to endorse their rods, something that I never did, as I was always convinced that sometime in the future I would become involved in the tackle trade. I didn't yet know how, but it was always in the back of my mind that it would be beneficial to establish my name as a trade name rather than to endorse other company's products.

I left the factory with two 13-foot carbon fibre beauties which I insisted on paying for despite the sweeteners promised by the 2 partners and stopped off at the River Nene on the way home. I couldn't help myself and would have blown several gaskets if I had waited even one minute longer without putting one of the rods through its' paces.

As beautifully perfect as she was in comparison with her glass fibre predecessors, there was still a problem; the top section threw the rod slightly out of balance. Jim Bruce had explained to me that the technology wasn't there to produce a tip in hollow carbon fibre that wasn't too stiff. There were no mandrels slim enough. His solution was to gradually phase out the carbon fibre and to intertwine the top 2 feet or so with glass fibre. This extra weight was the reason for the imbalance.

I suppose that it was a couple years later that Shakespeare offered a different solution to the problem with their President rod. Like the Bruce and Walker, the bottom half of the top section was hollow carbon and spliced into it was a slim insert of solid carbon - pretty much like a long quivertip.

This felt like a big improvement on the Bruce and Walker model, and as I tested the 13-foot model in the local tackle shop I was impressed - so impressed that I ordered 2 of them for the coming season, selling my two Bruce and Walkers to a friend.

Unknown to me at the time, the decision was to prove to be disastrous. The President turned out to be totally unsuitable for canal fishing.

The float would sail away, the strike made, and as the solid tip reached a certain point in its' curve, an astonishing flat spot appeared at the point of the splice, resulting in a kick that knocked every third fish off the tiny hooks that we were using. This knock wasn't quite so noticeable on rivers and lakes but coupled with light canal tackle it became a nightmare, and for the next couple of months I blew several matches on swims that were well capable of producing a winning weight.

Something had to change, and one day as I was explaining the problem to Barry Brooks, a big grin creased his face. "I've got just the solution Billy", he said. "But it will cost you". Barry was of course a Brummy tackle dealer and a member of the all-conquering Cofton Hackett and Birmingham national squad.

He then took out a new blank that he had begun to sell in his shop and handed it to me.

I was impressed, finally someone had managed to produce a carbon fibre rod with a hollow tip.

I ordered 2, unfortunately, Barry was as reliable as a Timex watch on a deep-sea diver, and it was to be several weeks before I eventually took delivery, in the meantime I became ever more frustrated with my President rod.

I collected the rods from Barry's shop on the Saturday evening, and with Mick Cotton and Bill Spragg in the car, drove down to a match on the Grand Union canal the following morning.

We had never seen Cassiobury park before, but it really was the most beautiful stretch of canal imaginable - somewhere South of Watford I believe, deep in southern woofter country.

I was quite disappointed with my swim. Parked all the way along the far side were dozens of big fishy barges; my swim was pretty open with a much smaller boat moored slightly to my left.

BEAUTIFUL CASSIOBURY PARK

The centrepin went onto one of the Brooksies and a fixed spool coupled with a peacock waggler onto the other. This was of course in the days before carbon fibre poles came out.

The small boat across from me rocked a little, and a chap climbed out holding in his hand a big bowl. He looked across at the row of anglers, smiled at me, and climbed back into the boat before emerging some 15 minutes later with his wife, and with a cheery wave they both disappeared into the park.

Shortly after, the starting whistle sounded, and my centrepin loaded Brooksie swung into action, while at the same time a pouchful of casters flew across the canal alongside the small boat. Perhaps half an hour later my breadpunch hadn't produced so much as a touch, and by now most of the anglers around me were casting alongside the boats.

So far, I hadn't seen a single fish caught - the canal flattered to deceive.

Down went the centrepin Brooksie and up came the fixed spool Brooksie. A single caster was slipped onto the 18's hook to a 12oz hook length, and the peacock waggler sailed serenely across the canal, barely having time to settle before disappearing under the boat before I even had time to strike.

One hook down.

Thinking that I had probably hooked a stray carp, I again tied on an 18's to a 12oz bottom, and once again, as soon as the tackle hit the water, I was taken completely by surprise; before I even had time to strike I was another hook down.

What followed next was one of my strangest ever angling experiences, accompanied by a story so implausible that it could not possibly be made up.

I was not only about to put my Brooksie through its paces, but I was also going to introduce it to a baptism by fire.

I was now stuck with a problem. Two casts and two hooks lost before I had even lifted the rod. These fish didn't know the rules and were prepared to play dirty.

I put the Brooksie down on the banking and thought about my options, in the meantime firing a pouchful of casters by the boat. Nothing broke the surface, but there appeared to be a slight agitation in the water.

*****

Now anyone who has ever travelled to the Florida Keys or the Caribbean islands in search of bonefish will understand the next bit.

You stand at the front of a shallow skiff, fly rod in hand, as the guide poles his way through little more than a foot of water when he suddenly bursts into life and says, "Cast - 20 feet - 10 o clock".

SEARCHING FOR NERVOUS WATER BONEFISH

No matter how hard you look, there is nothing to be seen in the crystal-clear water, nevertheless, you cast, and a hooked bonefish is often the result.

The bonefish is completely invisible to the untrained eye, its gleaming scaled mirror finish simply throwing back at you a reflection of the bottom - there is nothing to see even when it is almost at your feet.

What the guide has spotted is what they call "Nervous Water". This is no more than a slight irregularity in the wave pattern, completely indistinguishable among the rest of the waves without years of experience.

The water in front of my small boat at Cassiobury Park became "Nervous Water" whenever I fed the casters.

* * * * *

I tied on a 16s hook to a one-and-a-half-pound hook length, slipped on a double caster and cast over to the boat.

Within seconds the float shot under and disappeared under the boat.

This time I was ready for it, immediately plunging my Brooksie deep into the canal until only the reel was above the water, at the same time clamping down on the reel.

I could feel the rod strain and buckle under the water, but I held firm. Keeping my rod so far under the surface ensured that as the fish moved along the boat, the line stayed clear and didn't rub on the rough underside.

Maybe 20 nervous seconds passed, and slowly I felt the strain on the rod lessen; a few turns of the reel and I was now clear of the boat. I lifted the rod out of the water and less than a minute later a 2lb chub surfaced.

No one had mentioned chub at the draw, so I was pretty surprised. I once again lay the rod down on the banking, poured a cup of coffee and fed another pouchful of casters.

The water turned "Nervous".

The Ivan Marks' ten fish rule crossed my mind.

I was in no hurry and considered that after such a fish, a few minutes rest would help them to regain their confidence.

I suppose that a couple of hours had passed when Mick Cotton walked up to me. "Are you ready for off"? he said. "The bloody canal's barren, I haven't seen a single fish caught, me and Spraggy have packed up".

I was just resting the swim at the time, so I said, "I'll just have one more chuck, and if nothing happens, we're off."

The float buried - the Brooksie was buried - and soon a 2lb chub was in the landing net.

"How many of them you got?" Mick said, his mouth opening wide enough to engulf the fish.

"Lost count," I replied. "I think I might stick around for the weigh-in though."

It took several weighs on the canal scales, the final total being 29lb --15oz. One flipping ounce off a quite magical figure.

Had I used the same tactics with my Shakespeare President, its complete inability to assume a flexible, cushioning curve would have resulted in several breakages. My Brooksie had absorbed everything that the chub threw at it, and I did in fact finish the match with my original 16's hook.

*****

Now comes the real story.

I suppose that it was perhaps 3 or 4 years later, and I was once again in southern woofter country a couple of miles South of Cassiobury, when I noticed a chap walking up. He spoke to an angler a few swims away, who then pointed in my direction. Up walked the chap and spoke.

"You are Billy Makin," he said.

I was already aware of that, so I answered yes.

He went on. "Can you remember me waving at you a few years back when you fished opposite my boat at Cassiobury Park?"

I nodded.

"I believe that you had a good day with my babies?"

"Babies?"

He then told me the story.

Every morning after breakfast, he mixed up a big bowl of food, went to the side of his boat and fed the fish.

I remembered him carrying a bowl.

"They are so tame," he went on. "Sometimes they take pieces of bread or chips out of my hand."

I had caught 29lb --15oz on one pint of casters. What would I have caught if only I had brought a plate of chips to the match?

Every darn fish in the length gathered by the chap's boat at the same time every morning for breakfast, and who other than Golden Arm himself could possibly have drawn such a swim out of the 150 in the bag?

I had been well named for my prowess at the draw bag all those years earlier.

And the moral of the story????

I would guess that it is pretty conclusive proof that you can be both a Thai bar girl magnet - AND - lucky at the same time.

DAVE HARRELL – RIVER ANGLER SUPREME

I suppose Millsie got halfway there ---- poor Dave Harrell never made it out of the starting blocks - MIND YOU – he did know how to fish a bit.

CHAPTER 21

POLLY

I was hot, bothered, and feeling pretty frustrated when I finally found the match headquarters.

Some government cretin must have been browsing through a building catalogue selling roundabouts and had ordered 200 instead of 20.

I had just spent the last hour checking out every one of them.

I was somewhere in Milton Keynes and found myself waving at every passing concrete cow.

The occasion was the Wednesday sweep, and perhaps 60 or so anglers had turned up, the good news being that one particular angler hadn't.

Winning a match on the Grand Union canal was relatively easy for everyone, as you usually only had one man to beat - that man of course was Polly.

The first question at the end of every match was "What has Polly done?"

CANAL GROUNDBAIT FISHING WITH MARK POLLARD

AN ALL TIME GREAT

Mark Pollard's style of fishing was unusual, unorthodox, and should not have worked.

For a start, his rod was much too short, a kid's rod really - his casting technique involved an entanglement of arms and legs, coupled with passing the rod from one hand to the other, Ian Heaps style - his float was much too short and light - and his shotting pattern consisted of one micro shot down the line.

There's more.

He fished much too close to the far bank - he often left his line floating, even in a wind - and his feeding was all over the place, his catapult fed squatts covering half a tennis court.

It gets even worse.

His casting was all over the place and he cast far too often, never allowing his bait to settle.

In short, at a glance, Polly should never have won a sausage.

Now for those of you who regularly fished the squatt, you are probably now beginning to slot the jigsaw pieces into place, and to see how perfectly everything came together, also why the pole could not compete with the rod and line.

Mark's casting was all over the place because his loose fed squatts were.

His float was too short and too light so that he could search out areas only inches deep close to the far bank.

His use of one micro shot on the line, and his much too frequent casting meant that he always had a free-falling hookbait among his loose fed squatts, and his floating line kept his bait on the move, resulting in every inch of his swim being covered.

Polly kept piling up the wins, and together with a smashing bunch of lads fishing under either the Image or the Black Horse banner, became a force to be reckoned with wherever they fished.

Now I have to confess, the Mills and I tried to fish the Polly way, (using proper rods and proper floats) on many a practice session, and not on one single occasion did we ever make it work. We even tried swapping hands after each cast, until eventually, we both concluded that Polly caught fish despite the way he fished and not because of it.

The truth of course was not just in the technique that always seemed to work so perfectly, the secret was the man holding the rod - which ever hand it was held in.

So, how good was Mark Pollard in his youthful prime?

I would certainly place him in the top 5 most naturally talented match anglers that I ever had the privilege to fish with, possibly even vying with John Dean and Andy Findlay for the number one spot.

* * * * *

Back to the match and those flippin concrete cows and roundabouts.

The 60-peg match was split into 2 sections of 30, the high numbers being a couple of miles away on the Black Horse length, and being a none smoking, none drinking, none fornicating sort of God-fearing fellow, (err) I was pleased that God himself had once again guided my Golden Arm and benevolently blessed me with an end peg - number 30.

Let that be an important lesson to all you younger anglers - learn how to lie with a straight face.

Now at the time, most matches were being won with about 5lb, the method being waggler fished squatt close to the far bank.

I had in fact won the previous week's match having been drawn next to Bob Nudd, the waggler fished squatt proving marginally superior to the pole fished squatt on the day, even in the hands of the brilliant 4 times world champion.

It was usually possible to get a head start by fishing just past the rod tip for the first hour or so, but on this particular day the boats were up and down with the frequency of a Thai bar girl's unmentionables at a party, so the far bank was the only option.

My peg was different to all the others in that it wasn't a normal canal swim at all; I found myself sat on a concrete viaduct; the "pegger" having one leg slightly longer than the other, had mis-judged his distances, and not wishing to re-peg each swim had been forced to stick it in.

I tooled up and set about plumbing the swim.

This was like no other canal swim in the country.

By my keepnet, it was 6ft deep, as was the middle, and also tight against the far bank. Try to imagine a shoebox with no lid.

The whistle went for the off and having set my waggler slightly over depth, I cast across tight to the far concrete wall and fired in a few squatts.

Down went the float almost immediately, I struck - snagged on the bottom, as were the next 4 casts, no matter where in the swim my float landed.

Five hooks down in 10 minutes – one hour counting round-abouts - one hour waving at numerous concrete cows, and to cap it all I was now sat on top of a concrete snag pit.

A rather pretty girl smiled as her boat sailed by, and immediately my mood changed - life wasn't really so bad after all.

I tied on another hook and came a few inches off the bottom, re-cast, and a 1oz roach obligingly took my squatt.

This continued for the next near 5 hours, with the added bonus of an odd skimmer or two.

There were so many boats that day that everyone's swim was permanently like pea soup - mine was a lovely, fishy colour, not even an ounce of mud being stirred up by the propellers.

The reason?

Well, I was told after the match that when the viaduct was being built, the bottom and vertical sides were constructed of fibre glass and wire meshing. This, together with the depth of course explained the fishy colour and the hook losses.

There was no bottom mud for the boats to stir up.

Anyway, the fish went 12lb for what should have been an easy win.

It didn't quite work out that way.

I had strutted back to the headquarters, sticking out my chest like a rampant peacock on Viagra, confident that my 12lb would be more than enough - wrong.

The Black Horse bream had been partying and I wasn't even in the money.

It was a lonely drive home, a two-fingered salute greeting every passing concrete cow.

Something bothered me.

I was sure that I had left far more fish in the peg than had wound up on the scales, particularly as halfway through the match I had briefly latched onto something that felt suspiciously like a slab, but how was it possible to fish for them if every time I touched the bottom I lost a hook?

I thought about it all week.

The next Wednesday, everyone drawn in the low numbers was disappointed as the Black Horse bream had continued to party all week - I wasn't. I was once again drawn on peg 30, smack on top of the concrete viaduct and I had a cunning plan.

Out came my Bruce and Walker twelve-and-a-half-meter pole. I tied 10 feet of line to the elastic, attached a 16s hook, 12 inches above which was a small paternoster link and a swan shot.

I then set a 2-inch piece of peacock quill 8 feet deep in the 6-foot-deep swim, the theory being that the swan shot would not move with the flow and the peacock quill would present no tow on the shot as it would be lying flat.

Out went a pouchful of casters, and with double caster on the hook, the set up worked a treat - not once during the entire match did I get snagged.

Thirty minutes passed, then suddenly, the peacock quill cocked and slid gracefully away.

The elastic shot out, and a couple of minutes later a near 4lb slimy black beauty was in my keepnet.

I never really lined them up, occasionally going up to 30 minutes without a bite, and was as surprised as the scales man when ten slabs rattled the scales round to near 37lb.

The Black Horse bream had seen enough partying for the week and went totally absent for the day.

Why didn't Polly turn up?

It would have done him good to have been on the receiving end of a bloody good thrashing for a change and given him a reminder as to who was still the Governor round those parts.

Dream on Billy – dream on.

* * * * *

T'was early the next season that I was unfortunate enough to find myself on the receiving end of a jolly good rogering at the hands of Mark Pollard.

Sex was the primary cause, and Polly was positively revelling in the orgy that was unfolding before our eyes.

It was early July and Polly and I were sat next to each other on the Grand Union canal in a Luton AC open at Three Locks.

It had been a pretty cold few weeks leading up to the match which had delayed the spawning, and the sudden burst of hot weather had titillated the sex buds of tens of thousands of the canal's roach, and the canal's biggest ever gang bang was now underway.

Now you have to first visualize our two swims to understand what happened next.

My peg was a good one, in fact, for 364 days a year it was a potential match-winner, and Polly should have spent much of the 5-hour match watching me slide my net under a procession of bream.

It didn't quite work out that way, and the whacking great rush bed directly opposite me became the focal point for thousands of lusty roach, and the epicenter of the orgy to beat all orgies.

Polly's peg wasn't so good and had become little more than a waiting area for the thousands of roach impatiently queueing up in to get stuck into the action on the rush bed opposite me.

The whistle went for the all-in and immediately Polly was into fish under his rod tip.

My float stubbornly refused to budge more than once every few minutes, whilst Polly's float didn't even have time to get wet.

Fish were flying out every few seconds, entering Polly's net, and being unable to join in the action in front of me, they decided to have their own personal orgy in his net.

I had to do something pretty drastic as Polly was now piling up the pounds and the slaughter was becoming painful.

Over went the waggler against the offside rushes, and within seconds I was into a 2-pound bream.

"Look out Polly, I'm on your case," I shouted over. "You're in trouble now."

I should have kept my mouth shut.

Every cast after that produced either a small roach, a series of line bites, or multiple attempts to roger the float.

I have never seen fish in such a spawning frenzy before and would guess that the last thing on their mind when getting stuck in was a caster butty.

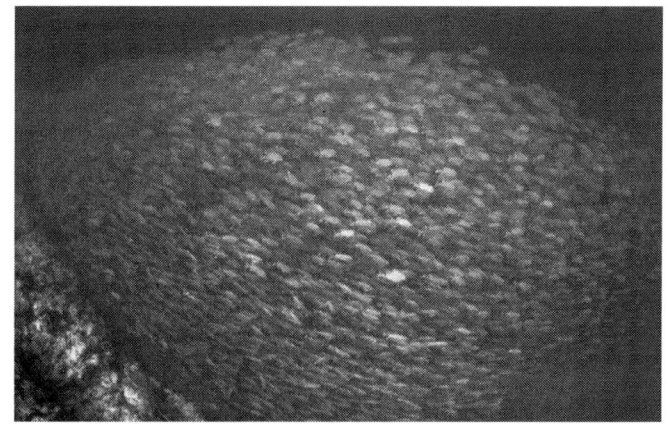

INSIDE POLLY'S KEEPNET AFTER 5 HOURS

Polly continued to catch every cast, and the gang bang in his net became every bit as hectic as the one opposite me, resulting in a pretty messy keepnet when he tipped his 14lb of roach onto the scales.

I think that I managed around 3lb of roach to go with my bream, and was just out of the main prizes, once again the spoils going to Mark.

A few weeks later I took a day off and drove down to Three Locks and sat at the same swim that I had drawn in the match - the result?

Forty flippin pound of bream.

Ah well, the Golden Arm at the draw bag was still working, it had just got the timing a little bit wrong.

CHAPTER 22

JACK

It's easy to name drop, isn't it?

I certainly do not have a problem doing it, especially when writing this series for Matchfishing and the book; I do however do it for a reason.

There are thousands of anglers out there who were around during my time on the open match circuit, and many of them will not only recognize the names that I often come up with but will themselves have been privileged enough to have both fished with and known the anglers themselves.

There is also another reason.

My time on the match circuit was, without doubt, "THE GOLDEN AGE OF MATCH FISHING", and the anglers I write about were the center stage actors.

Then there were the competitions themselves.

These were not just fishing matches, no sir, these were events of such national importance to all match fishermen that lifelong dreams were fulfilled, and immortality guaranteed.

These were competitions of such prestigious importance that sleeping the night before the event was near impossible, especially for a starry-eyed teenager who would be rubbing shoulders the next day with names that in many other sports would have had their pictures plastered across my bedroom walls.

Simply closing my eyes transformed a bleak Northern coal-mining town into a sparkling Kaleidoscopic landscape of sunlit countryside, as yet another match-winning bream slid over the landing net.

Visions of the trophy held high in triumph permeated and stimulated every sleeping fibre of my body, as Benny Ashurst, Billy Lane, and Ivan Marks stood in line to congratulate me.

A clout at the back of my head brought me back to reality.

"Wake up Makin and pay attention."

I reluctantly left the fish-filled swim, politely asked Benny, Billy, and Ivan to wait in line for another week, and was back in the school classroom listening to some boring history lecture.

I hadn't been chosen to fish the National - no sir, I had earned the right to fish by finishing leading points scorer in the 3, one hundred peg eliminators.

The competition was tough in those days, everyone wanted to fish the National, even Dad had failed to qualify, and being only 14 years old, the team captain had to check with the NFA that I could indeed fish.

I was in knee-trembling heaven.

The National Championship was most certainly the FA cup of match fishing, sadly, in years to come, its importance became watered down by two separate changes, the first one becoming quite obvious on the day that saw the introduction of more than one division, and the second one of course being the beginning of the points system that now decided the team placings.

It can quite reasonably be argued that under the points system the better teams took the lion's share of the spoils and led us into a more professional era - I do not disagree with this.

Sadly, along with this newfound professionalism came a corresponding loss of the intangible magic that made the competition so special.

A chill, almost uncontrollable shiver still runs through my body as I remember travelling halfway down the country at the age of 14 in order to fish our own FA cup on the Huntspill and the Kings Sedgemoor Drain, my whole system barely able to handle the adrenaline that was over-loading my schoolboy brain.

I could be the National Champion!

My team could be National Champions!

All I needed was a swim so full of big slab-sided bream that they didn't even have enough room to turn around.

We all knew that the Sedgemoor held such swims, and one man alone would lead his team to national glory, his name forever enshrined in the annals of angling history.

Several hundred anglers were heading in the same direction as was the battered old coach carrying our team, all thinking the same thoughts as mine, all on their way to achieving the same dream as mine.

This was an era of magic, a blank canvas just waiting for the brush of Cezanne, Da Vinci, Michelangelo, to paint the perfect landscape, with me, centerpiece, standing proud in triumph.

Only one man could fulfil that dream, and on the day that man was my old mate Dave Burr from Rugby.

Dave fought a thrilling peg for peg duel with Colin Clough of Coventry, a man who in later years also became a good friend, the outcome settling both the individual and team positions.

After the National came the Trent, the Welland, the Great Ouse, and the Staffordshire championships.

The BAA "Big Un" had a field of some 5000 anglers, that's right, count the noughts again.

Up't North we had the Northern Anglers Championships, a much sought-after title Dad once held, again a four-figure entry, while in the South there was the Thames championship and the LAA shield.

For all the present-day anglers who missed that golden era, you are truly unfortunate, great characters became household names, possibly even legends in fishing circles throughout the land, and perhaps the most noticeable change from modern-day "well known" match anglers, is that success and prestige were measured in titles won and not money.

It has to be said that the National Championship wasn't truly a test of a team's ability at the time of the one National, nor was the individual champion a "Super Star". In many ways it was pretty much a lottery settled by one man sat on a mountain of bream.

That was the magic.

The average club angler could fish against the greats of the era - the Benny's, the Billy's, the Ivan's, and if lady luck came calling, not just beat them, but also walk away with the most coveted title in world sport as far as I was concerned and achieve near-legendary status in their own town by that one moment of magic.

We had such a man back in Leigh when I was growing up.

Billy Hughes became the National Champion one year on the Witham and was treated with rock star reverence for many years afterwards.

* * * * *

I began the chapter by bringing up the issue of name dropping, and I make no apologies for mentioning the name Jack Charlton, a countryman and an excellent angler.

Like everyone in the land I was saddened by his death, particularly as Jack and I first became friends during the Golden Age of Match Fishing.

I first met Jack on the set of the BBC Hooked Championships in Northern Ireland, and as I was the reigning champion, I had to do a series of interviews with him before the series began.

We got on well, and never being one to allow fishing to get in the way of a good time, both Jack and I were usually "Last Man Standing" at the bar most evenings when everyone else had gone to bed.

The last day was classic Jack Charlton.

"The drinks are on me tonight lads." He said shortly after the final as we sat at the Bann View squash club, and so we got stuck in.

Jack was good for his word, and when the final bill for the night's carousing arrived, out came a signed photograph and a cheque book.

If the Bann View squash club is still standing, I will bet a pound to a penny that the signed photograph and the uncashed cheque are still on display on the club walls, as they are in dozens of pubs throughout Ireland.

Jack was a near God in the country thanks to the worldwide prestige that the Irish football team achieved under his management, and a signed photograph and cheque from Jack was more than equal to a knighthood back in England.

I very much doubt that anyone ever cashed a Jack Charlton cheque in the history of the country.

JACK CHARLTON

FISHERMAN AND WORLD CUP HERO

On the River Moy, at a town called Ballina in County Mayo, is the best salmon pool in the world. There are only 6 rods a day allowed to fish it and a waiting time of 2 years to even have a chance of fishing there.

Jack Charlton appeared at the pool one day and 6 Irishmen climbed out of the water and offered him their rod for the day, such was the reverence in which he was held in the country.

I spent a couple of treasured nights over a few beers with him during a pro-celebrity program that we were filming, but the last time that I saw him was on the banks of the Saint Helens Sankey canal at Newton.

It was a big-money match sponsored by the Post Office and Jack had been paid to do the presentation.

Halfway through the match, I had caught half a dozen small skimmers on the pole and the swim was now dead when Jack and his wife Pat walked along the towpath, Jack carrying a small folding chair.

Pat sat behind me on the chair, and we began talking, Jack not being his usual happy self.

"I gotta do something drastic, Jack," I said. "There's a thousand-pound first prize and 30 bob for second, I'm going to go for it."

Away went the pole and out came the waggler, the swim being some 20 meters wide. Over went a full half pint of maggots, followed by my waggler and a 16's hook baited with double maggot - this set up was big game hunting in the North West.

"I'm going to catch a carp in the next two minutes Pat," I said. I had seen the trail of bubbles arrive in the swim. "And Jack is going to hate handing over the cheque for 1,000 pounds."

"Good for you Billy," said Pat, just as the float sailed away, and 10 minutes later I slipped the net under an 8 lb. carp.

"Told you, didn't I?"

"How did you know that was going to happen?"

"Magic Pat," I said. "Just sheer magic."

Jack didn't seem too excited.

"What's up, mate?" I had to ask him, as Jack was never down.

"It's the football, Billy." Jack was still quiet as Pat spoke. "It's the politics at the club that's getting to him, he's even lying awake at night worrying about it."

"Get rid Jack," I said. "Don't kill yourself over bloody football, there's more to life than that."

"I've told him, Billy," Pat said. "He won't listen to me."

The headlines on the sports page of every newspaper in the country the next day.

> JACK CHARLTON RESIGNS AS MANAGER
> OF NEWCASTLE UNITED.

I kept my mouth shut.

Half a million angry Geordies could easily prove quite troublesome if any single one of them was to get wind of the previous day's conversation.

RIP Jackie old pal, and if you bump into any of my old fishing mates, let them know that I don't intend seeing them for quite some time.

CHAPTER 23

AH BERNADETTE

I suppose that the year would be around 1980, give or take one or two years on either side.

I was excited. I had just opened a letter inviting me to take part in the BBC angling championships under the series name of Hooked.

At the time, it genuinely appeared that match fishing was about to take off as a TV sport, and shortly afterwards I took part in a few Pro-Celebrity programs - more later.

The venue for the first series was to be Edgbaston reservoir around Birmingham, and as I had won a couple of matches there the previous year fishing caster and feeding long-range with casters in groundbait, I was pretty confident of not disgracing myself in front of the cameras; thoughts of winning it though were tempered by the shear quality of the field.

The big boys were out in force, and along with the rest of the country, Edgbaston was no longer a caster venue. The lake had fallen to the charms of the bronze maggot - any other bait being completely ignored by the quality roach that would be essential to winning.

The format of the tournament was relatively simple. Thirty

anglers had been invited, and 5 matches of 6 anglers were to be held, morning and afternoon. The winner of each match went through to the final accompanied by the fastest loser, giving a six-man final on the afternoon of the third day.

I had drawn in heat 5, so was due to fish the last match before the final. The opposition in my heat was formidable - positively knee-trembling - still, I had a punchers chance if I drew well.

I went along to the first match as a spectator to check out the form.

The match went entirely as expected, every weight coming on the bronze maggot fished at range under a waggler.

There was however one major flaw in proceedings; peg 1 was boxed into a tiny arm at the end of the reservoir and stood zero chance of qualifying - there was no room to work and no quality roach in the swim.

I had a feeling of deep foreboding about the swim.

I again went along on day 2, and as had happened in both the previous day's matches, bronze maggot at range took all the fish.

Peg 1 again threw up sweet Fanny Adams.

I didn't stay for the afternoon match, I had too much on my mind.

Peg 1 haunted my thoughts.

I just knew that the cursed bottle neck held my destiny in its barren depths and I had to come up with a game plan - something that no one else had tried in the other qualifiers.

I spent the entire afternoon and most of the evening wandering around the streams and ditches of Hinckley trying to scrape together enough bloodworm to give me a sporting chance if and when I drew the dreaded number 1 bottleneck.

The next morning, my hand went into the draw bag and out came peg 1.

Sod and his law can be a real pain in the nether regions sometimes.

The starting whistle sounded, and unlike the 5 angling superstars in my heat, I didn't toss out the waggler, instead, I fished canal style.

A dozen small roach on the bread punch, 20 or so on the pinky, followed by a decent run on the bloodworm came my way during the first hour. I wasn't exactly flying but the anglers to my right appeared to be struggling, so I kept my head down and continued plugging away at the small stuff.

Word came that Dave Thomas on the end peg was emptying it on the bronze maggot. I had no chance of beating him, still, there was the fastest loser spot to play for.

A TV camera appeared behind me, and a noisy and eternally smiling Bernard Cribbins waded into my swim and stood Microphone in hand inches from my float.

* * * * *

It was perhaps a couple of years later that I again met up with Bernard, who was both a comedian and comedy actor, having appeared in the Carry-On films and Fawlty Towers series. We had just finished a day's filming for a pro-celebrity series at Nottingham and were well into several noggins of free hotel drink provided by the TV company, accompanied by Vince Hill the singer, and Terry Biddlecombe the Jockey, when this gorgeous young female of around 25 appeared and introduced herself as Bernadette.

Terry's eyes grew large as he licked his lips and invited her to join us; he then spent the rest of the evening plying her with drinks and uttering some of the most outrageous chat up lines I had ever heard.

I would guess that it was around 2 in the morning when Terry suddenly keeled over, and being unable to stand up again, had to be half-carried to his room by Bernard and Vince, leaving me alone with the beautiful Bernadette.

"Would you like to learn how to catch gudgeon on the Oxford canal?" I asked.

"Love to", she replied. "What's your room number"?

She proved to be a willing pupil and positively swooned when I demonstrated my waggler technique.

Ah Bernadette - sweet memories.

*****

Now, where was I?

Ah yes - Bernard Cribbins had just waded into my swim, the notorious peg 1.

I had been having a decent run of fish and now Bernard was stood inches from my float.

He splashed forward and speaking into his mic said. "And here we have Billy Makin of Hinckley, how are you doing Billy?"

He then thrust the mic under my nose.

"I was doing very well Bernard until some blithering idiot waded into my swim." I replied.

He smiled - stepped back a few paces into the lake and said. "I think we will try that again Billy."

Again he stepped forward, this time making as much disturbance as he possibly could, and once again spoke into his mic. "And here we have Billy Makin from Hinckley, how are you doing Billy?"

I put on my best camera smile and replied in beautiful upper-class Queen's English. "Very well Bernard, I'm having a jolly good run of fish at the moment old boy."

He then clambered out of the water, gave me a wink and a big grin, then playfully slapping the back of my head said. "I knew you would see it my way sooner rather than later Billy."

Bernard Cribbins - Actor, Comedian, and Singer

I was now in queer street.

Dave Thomas already had the match wrapped up. The guy on peg 2 was beginning to catch a few and was now on the verge of over taking me, and there was I, sat staring at a swirling pool of mud courtesy of Mr bloody Cribbins.

I pulled a couple of loops of line off the centre pin and flicked my canal grey just beyond the mud cloud.

It barely had time to settle before I struck into a decent perch - a proper Billy Boston.

For the rest of the match, fishing the same line, I caught a small perch almost every chuck.

Up to that nice Mr Cribbins wading into my swim I hadn't even seen a perch. I can only assume that they were attracted by the disturbance and had come to investigate.

Decision time.

My net of canal tactics fish went just short of 5 lb, more than half of which had come immediately after Bernard had left the water.

This was 2nd in the match, and by a margin of one ounce, I was the fastest loser and had qualified for the final to be fished in a little more than 2 hours.

Without that wonderful man wading into my swim I would never have made it.

Better to be lucky than lovely.

* * * * *

There was one hour before the kick-off to the first ever angling equivalent of the FA cup.

The National Championships had by now become an out and out team event and little prestige was now attached to the individual champion.

I steadied myself - destiny beckoned.

My skeleton had left the closet; peg number 1 would never again darken my horizon.

My Golden Arm positively tingled as it plunged into the draw bag.

One piece of cardboard stuck to my fingers - it wouldn't let go.

I knew that this was the one for me.

I felt a pleasant stirring in my loins.

Ah Bernadette - sweet memories.

With trembling hands I opened the folded cardboard and breathed a sigh of relief.

Peg number 1 had moved on to another poor soul, I had drawn number 4.

I was well pleased with being in the middle of the mini-match length as I had noticed a pattern emerging over the previous 2 days. The morning match favoured pegs 5 and 6 as the fish gradually moved into the feeding area - the afternoon match (same pegs), favoured the middle to lower numbers.

I had a cunning plan, hatched out the previous evening after I had returned cold, wet, and exhausted from several hours of bloodworm scraping.

Having closely studied three of the four previous matches, I noticed that on many occasions, the anglers were coming back with a burst or shredded maggot without having seen a bite.

This spelt one thing only to me - the fish were intercepting the bait on the drop, and the peacock quill wagglers were not sensitive enough to register this.

This was to be the edge that I had been searching for.

I had the perfect tool for the job - a float that I had been working on to solve a similar problem that I had found at Kingsbury Gravel pits.

Instead of the peacock waggler used exclusively by the rest of the field, my waggler was a 3-stage construction.

The base consisted of a small balsa body into which was inserted some 6 inches of neutral buoyancy cane, not much thicker than a toothpick, and sitting on top of the cane was a small balsa sight bob.

The simplicity of the set up was its beauty.

An AAA shot either side of the float sunk the balsa body, at which point 6 inches of cane sat proud of the water.

Down the line were 2 dust shot spread well apart, each one sinking the cane stem some 3 inches until only the tiny balsa sight bob was visible.

Now for the anglers among you, I am sure that now you can see quite clearly through the plan; not only could I see every drop bite, but I was also about to adapt my entire feeding regime to encourage them.

The whistle blew for the all-in.

Five peacock wagglers sailed out followed by 5 pouchfuls of bronze maggots.

My waggler stayed dry, instead, I played around with canal tactics as I catapulted small numbers of bronze maggots with twice the frequency as the rest of the competitors.

Wayne Swinscoe grinned sympathetically at me as he slipped his net under his second quality roach. Dickie Carr, a couple of pegs away, was beginning to show.

DICKIE CARR WAS BEGINNING TO CATCH

One hour into the match and it was now time for me to make my move.

Unlike the other 5 swims, mine had been rested - the fish should now be confident, more importantly, they should be looking skywards for the next meal - a meal that was being delivered on a 20-second timeline.

Out went the bodied waggler.

It sat proud for some 5 seconds, then slowly sank to half its length as the first dust shot settled.

I counted to 5.

The second shot didn't come into play.

I struck, and my first half-pound roach was in the net.

Wayne looked anxiously across - I winked.

My theory had proved correct, I now had to establish a rhythmic feeding and casting pattern in order to keep the fish up in the water.

Try to visualise this pattern.

I fed half a dozen maggots - waited 20 seconds, and again fed another half a dozen.

I now waited some 5 seconds for the maggots to partially sink, then I cast into the middle of the feed pattern, trying to get my bait to sink among the feed bait.

Almost every fish that I caught came on the drop, the float

doing the job I had designed it for to perfection.

WAYNE BEGAN TO FALL BEHIND – DICKIE PUSHED ME ALL THE WAY

I had come through my greatest test, and as I was the reigning Matchman of the Year, I now held 2 of the 3 most sought-after titles in match fishing.

I was growing in confidence - I felt unbeatable.

Unknown to me - in a far-off land - in a distant far-flung corner of a once-proud empire that encompassed half the globe, a dark cloud was forming in a town close to Mansfield.

The cloud grew in both its size and malevolence, and gathering malicious intent, moved in my direction, consuming everything in its path.

That dark cloud was known as John Dean - a name that in years to come would sit comfortably among the likes of Saddam, Osama, Les Prust, and Vlad the Impaler.

An unholy alliance was formed with Maxi Winters, and the next year Mad Max and John Dean stole both of my titles, once again relegating me to the ranks of the also-rans. I was destined to ply my trade whittling pieces of balsa into canal greys, and to dig holes in Mother Earth; holes that were to be filled with water and stocked with the unholy abominations known as carp - the all-conquering spawn of Lucifer - Beelzebub's buddies - Satan's soulmates.

I was soon to become an outcast from society - a pariah - eternally condemned for destroying a once-great sport.

Still ---- I had my memories, and what memories they still are.

Ah Bernadette - such sweet, sweet memories.

CHAPTER 24

FLASH

John Bloor was an early pioneer of commercial fisheries and took on Meadowlands lakes on the outskirts of Coventry, where through sheer hard work, he turned the lakes into an excellent fishery before selling up, and along the way helped me a lot at my Wolvey lakes.

John was a real grafter, and several times a year he came to net my lakes in order to help to balance the stocking level, removing thousands of horny roach that simply would not stop copulating.

This was no mean feat, as John had a bad back, so I gave him all the encouragement possible from the sidelines as he painfully hauled in the net, at times having to lie down to relieve the pain.

I felt his pain and told him to get up and get on with the job and stop moaning.

As Meadowlands improved, the anglers began to flock in, so John set up a little food stall to be run by his lovely wife Janet, who I always called Mrs McEnroe.

Now it has oft' been rumoured that occasionally, I can be a taker of the Michael, Mrs McEnroe being one of my favourite targets.

Every week I would phone her and give her the number of people admitted to Walsgrave hospital with food poisoning that week as a result of eating her burgers.

One day I turned up at Meadowlands to see John and asked the good lady for a burger.

She glared, said something extremely unpleasant, and fried up the burger which was then served on a nice white serviette.

"Not one word or I will hit you with the frying pan," came the threat.

I smiled condescendingly, and proceeded to demolish the burger, making all the appropriate yums and chomps, accompanied by much lip licking.

"Delicious", I said, "absolutely fabulous, the best burger I have ever eaten".

Mrs McEnroe was delighted.

I then reached into my pocket and took out a box of Rennies, emptied the entire contents into my hand, and stuffed the lot into my mouth, chomping and crunching them in front of her.

Mrs McEnroe turned red and reached for the frying pan.

It was perhaps 2 weeks later that I had to pop over to Meadowlands again to see John.

Mrs McEnroe shot daggers from her eyes.

"One of your delicious burgers please".

"Bugger off".

"Please, please, I promise no more tricks, and I won't say a word".

"If you do, I will wrap this frying pan around your head".

Five minutes later, the burger was served on a neat white serviette, and Mrs McEnroe stood awfully close, pan in hand.

"Ketchup and mustard please".

She passed them over, pan still in hand, and stood open-mouthed as I neatly squirted both ketchup and mustard all around the outside of the burger.

I then picked up the burger, threw it into the bin, and ate the serviette.

On yer bike Billy boy

NOT A PRETTY SIGHT

John and I quickly moved away from an enraged Mrs McEnroe and ran off, followed by a stream of obscenities that I dare not repeat.

Mrs McEnroe didn't speak to me for weeks after.

I really can't think why.

* * * * *

I would guess that being a Micky taker was something that I inherited from my dad, he was pretty much the same and had a lifelong battle with Dickie Bowker of Leigh.

Dickie, along with his son Richard, was a superb angler and could talk the hind legs off a donkey.

I well remember the two of them being peg for peg and matching each other fish for fish during an evening sweepstake at Runcorn. Dickie pipped dad by ounces, dad always claiming that Dickie's constant chatter cost him the match.

The tables were turned during a good-sized Open at Hawkes lake, Wem, in Shropshire.

Dad and Dickie were again peg for peg on a narrow peninsular, separated by a thick bush, neither of them able to see each other. They could however speak, as being on a point they were only around 5 yards apart.

The area was poor with only a section to fish for, Dickie being the only one to catch during the first couple of hours.

Dad then caught a tiny perch.

"What's geet Makin?'

"A big Billy." came the reply.

Dad left it for 10 minutes or so, then splashed his landing net in the lake.

"Hast geet another Makin?'

"Sure have Bowker, another big Billy."

For the rest of the match, dad repeated the charade every 10 minutes or so.

Dickie couldn't shut up and told everyone within earshot that Makin was emptying it.

Come to the weigh-in, Dickie tipped his potential section winning 3 roach back and stood behind Dad.

The ensuing verbal assault when dad pulled out his net to reveal a section winning half-ounce perch is unprintable.

This genetically inherited problem has afflicted me for most of my life and came into play during one of Pat O'Connor's opens at Nell's bridge on the Oxford canal.

I was drawn in Death Row, the first section up from the bridge.

Never in history has anyone ever had so much as a bite in this section, and true to form, two hours into the match no one had had a bite.

Dave Duggan on the next peg to me went for a walk - Lucifer nodded.

I swung in Dave's pole rig and added an extra dust shot to his mini-bulk, at the same time bursting his bloodworm before returning it to the swim.

Dave returned and swung in his tackle.

'I've had a bloody bite." He shouted.

He re-baited and swung out his rig again.

His pole float settled for a few seconds then sank, ever so slowly.

Dave struck.

"Damn" came the response. "I've just missed a bite."

There was a 20 quid section prize at stake, so Dave settled in.

For the next half hour, Dave's float disappeared every single cast, each time resulting in a series of unprintable profanities.

It was only when he noticed the anglers around him near falling off their tackle boxes that he clocked the problem.

"Makin you little "bounder", I'm going to kill you." Seems to be close to what came out if I remember correctly.

Why did he pick on me?

I always seemed to get the blame whenever things went wrong, I have already mentioned the time I emptied chrysoidine dye into the coffee container when I was working at British Gas.

All hell broke loose, the entire office turned yellow - the screams from the secretaries could be heard half a mile away.

Again, why did people point in my direction - I simply didn't fancy coffee that morning - I wasn't thirsty - that's why I was the only one still white.

* * * * *

Occasionally, my sense of humour bordered on the reckless.

One fine Summer's day as I was sat in the house wondering where to go fishing in the afternoon the phone rang.

Panic set in as the voice on the other end mentioned the dreaded words "Customs and Excise."

'Is that Billy Makin?"

I considered denying it and was about to tell the voice that I was his brother and Billy was on holiday in Alice Springs, when the voice explained that the Government controlled, legalized Mafia mob for whom he worked, wanted to arrange a corporate day down my fishery.

I breathed a sigh of relief and a date was arranged.

I was off the hook, but the thought of 100 Customs and Excise men descending on the village of Wolvey presented multiple problems, for not only would they be fishing a one-day match, but there would also almost certainly be a week's intensive practice for most of them, many of whom would be staying locally.

The locals would lynch me.

This would devastate the local economy, as Bulkington, the next village, was home to a couple of characters who lived on the dark side of the law - the benefits of their personal version of free enterprise being enjoyed by all the neighbouring villages, especially a wealthy village like Wolvey - the local coppers included.

Few people bought cigarettes and tobacco at the going rate, even the vending machines at the local pubs were stocked almost exclusively with contraband brought in from the continent, and virtually every bottle of alcoholic spirits had made the voyage from somewhere overseas.

The local currency was the fiver. No one ever dealt in ten-pound notes, only fivers.

I will explain.

A regular visitor to my lakes was a chap whose name I will not mention, so I will call him Flash.

Now Flash was very wealthy, having just sold his business for 5 million quid, and Flash liked to let people know how wealthy he was.

As he was quite young, he soon got bored and became very friendly with a chap from Leeds who had created an ingenious, modified version of a photocopying machine. The end product was as near perfect as was humanly possible, and once the right paper was sourced, anything was possible, the finished article being completely undetectable by the human eye.

Flash started with Euros. One hundred pounds bought you 500 quid's worth of near-perfect Euros, and soon, Bulkington village became a ghost town, the inhabitants spending most of the year in Spain, returning many times with a suntan and considerably more than their original 100 quid, with which they bought even more Euros.

Flash moved on to car tax discs.

Most people in the area were now sporting 10 quid tax discs (That was the going rate), and 100 Customs and Excise men were due.

Flash then tried fivers.

PERFECTION

They were perfect, the tills of the local shops and pubs being stuffed with fivers and little else.

Our little Warwickshire enclave had its own currency.

Everything worked perfectly, and whenever we found ourselves with too many fivers, we simply paid them into the bank - no one ever noticed.

Flash continued to fish my lakes almost daily, buying food and bait in great quantities, always paying with fivers.

One day, I was having a quiet drink with Bob, the landlord down at the Axe and Compass pub in the village, when Flash walked in, having parked his spanking shiny new red Mercedes Sports directly in front of the entrance for everyone to see.

He couldn't help himself from buying us all a drink, in fact, several drinks – paid for in fivers of course - and he continued drinking bucket loads of expensive single malt.

Bob didn't mind the fivers; they would all disappear in someone's change.

After a hectic session, and completely unable to walk in a straight line, he staggered out and drove off in his Merc ending up in a ditch alongside the A5.

The breathalyzer went off the scale and the magistrate imposed a massive fine and a two-year driving ban.

I suppose that it would be a couple of weeks later as I was having a few drinks in the Blue Pig in Wolvey village when in walked Flash, and once again bought everyone a drink, needless to say, paying in fivers.

When he went to the toilet, I grabbed a book of raffle tickets from Mick, the landlord, and on returning Flash looked at the tickets.

"Do you want to buy one Flash?" I asked. "They are only one pound each."

He then took out a wad of fivers a couple of inches thick and handed me 4 of them.

"Give me 20," he said, in a voice loud enough for the entire pub to hear.

I handed over 20.

"What's the first prize then Bill?"

"A brand-new Mercedes Sports car," I replied, as I pocketed the money.

"I've already got a Merc Sports," he said.

"Yes, I know Flash, that's the first prize, you won't be needing it for a couple of years."

Believe it or not, he took it the right way and told me to buy everyone a drink with the money.

These dodgy fivers were now the main currency in the village - the vending machines were full of dodgy fags - everyone was driving around with dodgy tax discs - half the village was on holiday in Spain spending their brand-new dodgy Euros, and 100 Customs and Excise men were due to descend on us in a couple of weeks.

I was in trouble - was that a rat I could smell?

One hundred Customs and Excise men?

Why had they chosen to surface in Wolvey?

Something didn't smell right.

I spent the next few days mentioning it in the local pubs, both in Wolvey and Bulkington, and by the day of the match both villages had once again returned to the accepted legal standard.

Fivers disappeared, expensive fags filled the vending machines, brewery spirits filled the pub shelves, and cars were parked in garages rather than on drives.

The fateful day arrived.

Following the usual superb breakfast at the Axe and Compass, I presented the organizer with the invoice for a corporate day – 1,000 pound plus 175-pound (17.5%) VAT.

A fat git with a red face grabbed the invoice and remarked, "The agreement was 1,000 pound - that should have included the VAT."

"Sorry mate," I replied. "You lot make the rules, not me, it's 1,000 pound PLUS 17.5% VAT."

'YOU'RE ON MY PATCH NOW." His voice was threatening. "This doesn't end here."

With that, the red-faced, fat git stormed off.

* * * * *

At one minute to 10, I was stood at the high point between lakes 5, 4, and 2, the three lakes that I had pegged, holding my volume controllable megaphone ready to shout the "all in" when there was a sudden ear-shattering clap of thunder.

I couldn't resist it and turned up the volume to its' max.

'"EVEN GOD HATES YOU B--------S". My voice boomed.

I was just about to shout the "all in" when I noticed Fat Man on lake 4.

I ambled unassumingly behind him, and with the volume still on max, stuck the megaphone inches from his ear and bellowed "ALL IN".

FULL VOLUME

He near shit himself and fell off his basket onto his box of maggots which disappeared into the lake.

Come to the weigh-in, I walked along lake 4 with Geoff, my bailiff, writing down the weights as Geoff did the weighing.

Fat man pulled out his net and tipped his fish onto the scales, the needle swinging round to 18 pounds; he then emptied his fish back into the lake.

I pretended to write down the weight, at the same time saying in a loud voice, "Fat Man - 15 pounds."

"It bloody well wasn't." Fat man almost screamed, his red face turning purple in fury. "It was 18 bloody pounds."

"Fifteen pounds," I repeated. "Eighteen pounds less 17.5% VAT is fifteen pounds - that's all you're having - YOU'RE ON MY PATCH NOW."

Oh, Dad - what a genetically perverse legacy you have left me with.

* * * * *

I suppose that it was a couple of months later, and Flash was in a Burbage pub doing business with Tripod, the landlord.

Tripod ran his own fishing club and most of the fivers invariably ended up down my lakes.

Tripod was so named because people who saw him in the shower thought that he had 3 legs. His wife seemed to have a permanent limp and always walked around with a dreamy smile on her face.

Tripod handed over 1,000 pounds in genuine tenners, and Flash handed him 3,000 in dodgy fivers.

The Customs and Excise men swooped.

At exactly the same time, just as Mr X was unloading an entire pantechnicon of illegal fags and booze in a Bulkington barn, they also swooped.

Flash and Mr X kept each other company for the next 2 years in Birmingham's Winston Green nick.

PORRIDGE FOR FLASH

I in turn received a visit from the VAT man - oh shit.

The guy turned out to be a keen match angler, and we spent most of the day in the Blue Pig pub in the village, and one way or another, he managed to get me a rebate on the previous year's accounts.

MY LOCAL IN WOLVEY VILLAGE

It's good to have friends in low places.

As for the box of fivers buried in my back garden - they were day ticket money from my lakes which I had to slowly recirculate in the local supermarkets and petrol stations.

Where else would I have got them from? Half the people who fished the lakes paid in dodgy fivers.

I needed a long holiday.

Spain looked good, besides, I had 2 grands worth of brand-new Euros to get rid of, bought from Flash one evening when he was drunk down at the Blue Pig, and paid for with 500 quid's worth of his own dodgy fivers.

Oh Dad, what have you done to me? - Speak to you tonight when I'm asleep.

CHAPTER 25

A STRANGE CONCEPT

"You lucky (Bounders)", came the voice over John Harvey's phone. "God, I wish I was there with you instead of this rat-hole."

I recognized the voice, John passed me the phone, and sure enough, there was my old mate Tony Lock on the other end looking and sounding extremely sorry for himself.

I hadn't seen Tony for close on a year now since the last match over here in Thailand, and thanks to our little virus friend, Tony was trapped in England with little chance of re-joining our match group for months to come.

We were at Big Joes' lake and just weighing in after our morning session. This was to be followed by a couple of beers at the headquarters, much rivalry banter, and then an afternoon session.

Strange, eh?

A break halfway through a match and then a second half.

John, Dennis Dixon, and I were separated by ounces, each of us having a little over 20lb.

I held the camera phone recording the weigh-in and poor Tony was forced to watch proceedings.

Owing to the time difference, it was still early morning in England and Tony was preparing for a match at Redhill.

Are you still fishing at "Joe Bloggs" lakes?" I asked. (I have changed the name so as not to upset the owner).

"No," came the reply. "What's the point? You draw your peg and decide whether or not to fish. Half a dozen swims will throw up over a hundred pound and the rest of the field will struggle for a bite."

My mind wandered back to a Saturday canal match on the Oxford cut where I was drawn next to Frank Barlow.

"Where you off to tomorrow, Frank?" I asked.

I'm on the bleedin Dove," came the reply. "I've fished it 7 times over the last couple of years and haven't had one single bite yet."

I knew the feeling well, having had 5 match blanks on the trot on the same river over a similar time frame.

I read the Angling Times a few days later and Frank had broken the 100lb barrier.

OK, so where is this chapter heading?

Well, let me give you an imaginary scenario.

There is a golf tournament and 50 of the world's top golfers are present together with 5 amateur hackers.

If you only have 5 golf balls to play with and you give one of them to each of the hackers, they will take the first 5 places and the 50 Pro's will all draw a blank.

Match fishing can be a little like this.

It is a double-edged sword.

Its beauty is that a hacker (No disrespect meant) can compete with the world's finest angler and beat him.

Its downfall is that unlike any other sport that I can think of, the finest exponent of that sport can easily come last and the worst sportsman in the field can easily win.

Match fishing is unique among the world's sports, and if people are happy with the way Lady Luck often determines the outcome, then there is no need to change anything.

There is however another way.

A way that allows all the golfers to have a ball and not just the lucky few.

* * * * *

I will tell you about the worst match that I have ever fished, a match that was so bad that my brief resurrection as a fisherman after a 30-year break, once again almost came to an inglorious end.

John Harvey had arranged for the 4 of us, Lee had joined our party, to travel to Bangkok to fish against the Thai match anglers Thai style.

We stayed overnight in the Thai capital, and after a noggin or two at an English style pub drove to the match venue the next morning to find ourselves horrified at both the venue and the rules.

Worse was to come - much worse.

We were all pegged 3 meters apart with one exception; my swim was that exception.

ENOUGH SAID

As we were at the end of the pool, the last 3 swims were squeezed in and I had exactly 2 metres to the Thai anglers on either side of me.

Rule 1 - bread-based feed and hook baits only.

Rule 2 - no feeding by hand or catapult.

Rule 3 - maximum pole length of 5 metres.

I had 5 metres of a pole lent to me by Alf, with a small cup on the end to feed with.

Rule 4 - 2 hooks were allowed.

I was ready for home long before the whistle blew for the off.

My range limit was 5 metres with the English style set up, the Thais on either side of me could fish with their whips close to 9 metres by using a long line.

I could only feed at 5 metres, not so the Thais.

By using a strange separation technique, they were able to mould a ball of groundbait around the top hook, accompanied by a small piece of paste around the bottom one.

My float sat motionless at 5 metres, as the Thais 2 metres either side of me and fishing at 9 metres, had me completely boxed in, and proceeded to catch small carp and goldfish, occasionally coming out with 2 fish at a time.

I had to endure 2 hours of this torture and was glad when the half time whistle sounded.

A couple of beers later, I reluctantly wandered back to my tiny pocket of bank space to resume the pain, lasting perhaps 15 minutes before I completely cracked and returned to the bar.

The other side of the lake was a little more productive, and John, enjoying a full 3 metres and 17 centimetres of bank space managed to wangle out some 8 pounds of goldfish to win the match, beating Krick, the Thai angling superstar, by a considerable margin on the next peg.

Horrible - horrible - horrible waste of a day for Dennis, Lee, and myself.

OK, so let's cut to the chase.

The venue was a concrete oblong - imagine a large swimming pool where every swim is the same depth, as indeed it was.

There were no features and no bonus fish and as far as I can gather it only contained small carp and goldfish.

Can you now see where this article is heading?

It may seem like hell to someone who is used to having a smooth chub and barbel filled glide on the Wye or Dove, but to someone who has to fish the same match on a swim containing sod all against a man on a shed load of big chub, you have to admit that the concept does have some merit.

Every golfer has a ball, not just the 5 novices, and the absence of fish-holding features ensures that no one drives away straight after the draw because of a bad peg.

There ARE no bad pegs - every peg is equal.

I know that this is not every match anglers' cup of tea, but as silly as it sounds, Ray Mills, Mick Cotton, and I had some great times during the enforced closed season many years back sat around my tiny garden pond, 2 metres apart, catching gudgeon with a side stake of a few bob.

*****

When I originally set up Phases 3 of Makin Fisheries, the design was to make every swim the same depth and the same width. Initially, it worked a treat and the anglers loved it.

The fish began to grow too quickly, so I banned pellets to slow down the rate of growth and to a certain extent it worked.

Carp, however, do like eating and you may be able to slow down the rate of growth, but you can never really get on top of it.

Fisheries have tried to go down the route of silverfish only, but for some reason, silvers thrive much better in the carp waters. They are also much more susceptible to constant handling and can easily switch off for months on end.

Unlike the various species of carp, silvers do not want to be 20lb by tomorrow and therefore feed less often.

What certainly happens is that as carp grow bigger, hotspots emerge, resulting in the situation that Tony had mentioned.

This of course has created the absurd situation where in some waters, the average size of the fish is now approaching double figures, and any form of finesse disappeared long ago to be replaced by hooks more at home in a butcher's shop, pole elastic thick enough for bungy jumpers, and poles so strong that they could easily be used by pole vaulters.

The only answer to this problem is a hybridized fish (F1's are a step in the right direction), or a complete drain down with all fish removed followed by a re-stocking with small fish every couple of years.

This is what happens on the concrete bowl that we fished in Bangkok.

Realistically, there has to be a middle way.

The concept however does have merit and with sensible pegging and fishery rules it can be made to work.

The question is of course: -

Would match fishing be the same if we took away the element of luck?

It never really made any difference to me.

I was one of the hackers who always got a ball.

That was why I used to have the nickname Golden Arm, because of my uncanny ability at the draw bag.

There isn't one single bush or reedbed on the entire Oxford Canal that I haven't drawn at least once.

Looks and luck - what a combination - eh?

As Napoleon said, "Give me lucky generals rather than good ones."

CHAPTER 26

DECISION TIME

Throughout the book I have purposely avoided any form of instructional material, my reasoning being that as I have been away from match fishing for near 30 years, I am in no position to write about a match scene that is so obviously different to the one that I left - the world has moved on and so have match fishing techniques.

However, I am going to try something a little different to my normal format.

No matter how much fishing has changed, fish haven't, so firstly I will explain a 3-day match fishing spree that pretty much altered the course of my life.

* * * * *

The day was a Saturday close to 30 years ago and I was staring in horror at my swim on the Trent.

It was 8 foot deep, belting through, full of boils, and as the river was pretty much a bronze maggot job, any maggot thrown in would not be reaching the bottom within the next 100 yards.

In short, the swim was unfishable with a float, and as I had neither feeder rod nor one single feeder in my entire angling collection, an early bath was definitely on the cards.

I sat down and studied the swim for a few minutes. There was no reason for the fish not to be there, and as I had come fourth on the river the previous week, beaten by 3 men chucking out a big feeder, I was determined to sort out the problem.

Out came my 17-foot canal rod together with my centrepin reel, and on went the biggest stick float in my box, accompanied by a great lump of shot some 2 foot above the hook and a no 6 dropper one foot away.

Now for the feeding.

I mixed up a bowl of brown crumb into which went a pint of casters, and every swim down, in went a tiny rock-hard ball that shot straight to the bottom and would I guess, roll down the swim, breaking up and releasing the casters as it did so.

The stick float was seriously over shotted and held back by the slowly revolving centrepin so that it travelled at half pace through the swim.

It worked, in fact, not only did it work, I finished 4th in the 200-peg match from what had initially appeared to be an unfishable swim, and once again I was beaten by 3 men tossing the plastic pig out into the middle of the river.

As I drove home, pretty darn pleased with myself, the realization suddenly hit me.

I would never again win a match on the Trent, nor would anyone else unless they were prepared to toss out a whacking great feeder and spend 5 hours gazing skywards.

River fishing was coming to an end, and as more and more matches were won on the feeder, more and more anglers would begin fishing it.

The 54lb Trent match record (please excuse the boasting) that I once held was regularly being beaten, often doubled by massive bags of chub and bream, all taken on the feeder.

That was on the Saturday.

Sunday found me sat opposite a boat on the Shropshire Union Canal at Norbury junction. It wasn't a good area, but the boat gave me an outside chance of catching an odd bonus fish.

Ten minutes before the match began a chap appeared on the boat. He was a pleasant enough fellow and apologized for disturbing my swim, informing me that he had a small job to do and would be gone in a few minutes.

The whistle went, and as my small peacock waggler flew delicately across the canal, he struck up his welding torch.

The float did not land feather-like alongside the boat as was intended.

It went over the boat, halfway across a field, and embedded itself in a hawthorn bush.

I was blinded as I had been facing directly into the flash.

I tried to re-tackle but couldn't get the line through the rod rings.

It was a good 3 hours before I could see well enough to drive home.

And so we come to Monday.

Monday was always my lifeline.

Monday evening in Summer meant Mallory Park, and even an average swim could throw up double figures of skimmers fishing caster on the waggler and feeding balls of groundbait filled with whatever bait had been left over from the weekend.

I loved Mallory Park, and like every one of the regulars, was not well pleased when Roy Marlow stuck a load of carp in the lake.

ROY MARLOW WITH IVAN, HIS BUSINESS PARTNER

I was pegged next to Nicki, Roy's son, still a teenager and a pretty decent angler.

Out went my waggler followed by a couple of balls of feed, and with much effort and grunting, out sailed Nicki's enormous feeder full of boilies into the middle of the 100-yard-wide lake.

Nicki had six bites in the two-and-a-half-hour match and landed 6 carp for 35 pounds, all on a hair rigged boilie.

And so ended 3 rather career-defining days.

Both Mallory Park and the Trent were no longer float fishing venues, and years of learning the art of casting and feeding on the canals had also been negated, in fact, often completely obliterated by a 15-meter lump of carbon fibre with a feeding cup on the end.

It was time to adapt or to walk away from the sport.

I chose the latter course of action that very Monday evening.

That was almost 30 years to the day, and I have never fished a match since the end of that 3-day spell, nor have I ever even had the slightest inclination to do so.

Well, catching whacking great monstrosities here in Thailand, coupled with ample supplies of ice-cold beer doesn't really count, does it?

CHAPTER 27

SPONSORSHIP

I was sat in my Pattaya apartment here in Thailand flicking through Facebook when I noticed a post by John Harvey on a site that appears to have a readership of thousands of current and lapsed match fishermen. A company called PLANTATIONS INTERNATIONAL were ploughing a few thousand pounds into a sponsored match on a couple of local lakes less than 30 minutes' drive from where I live here in Thailand.

FISHING WINS – SPONSOR WINS

This set the juices flowing, it also presented many problems.

Not only had I not fished for almost 30 years, but the only tackle in my possession was fly tackle, consisting of rods, reels, and lines suited to my frequent trips to Florida and the Bahamas in the days when I was earning a bob or two, and wives and girlfriends were content with a couple of quid a week and not 50% of everything that I owned.

Now living over here in Thailand are many lapsed, and in many cases still functioning veteran UK matchmen. Added to these are hundreds of UK based match fishing dinosaurs who visit the fleshpot that is Pattaya every year to remind themselves of what life used to be like before 3 square meals a day of Viagra and chips was required to rekindle a long-lost teenage response.

The miracle life-enhancing drug helps to bring back memories of past glories and conquests, resulting in the unexpected excitement and enthusiasm of an 18-year-old catching his first glimpse of an upper thigh, and maybe even the odd whisp of foliage.

I digress, so back to the fishing bit.

As I run a couple of bars, many of the old matchmen pop in to have a drink and a chat, before disappearing with a takeaway bride.

For those not familiar with Pattaya, a takeaway would usually be aged between 18 and 30.

Now blackmail is a dirty word, and I assure you that all the match tackle that I rapidly acquired was given completely voluntarily.

* * * * *

Before I go into the actual fishing, as this was to be a sponsored competition, I feel that I have to be critical of the sponsorship that is currently available in the world of fishing.

Other than a few exceptions, sponsorship has been virtually non-existent outside of the fishing tackle trade, the reason for this I put firmly on the shoulders of the fishing weeklies.

To give you an example of their complete lack of knowledge of how sponsorship works, I ran the Winter League at my fishery and Preston Innovations threw in 5000 pounds in prize money. The league was so popular that the 20 teams of 12, (240) anglers was not enough and the second league of 20 teams had to be created with Dave Preston throwing in another 5 grand.

Every one of the 12 matches paid out 1000 pound to each of 3 zone winners with a couple of grand to the overall winner.

This was every week for 12 weeks during Winter, matches occasionally being fished through holes in the ice.

So Dave's investment was 10 grand, and it is fair to say that a little bit of promotional coverage by the angling press for what was effectively their league would have been appreciated by Dave.

Personally, I wasn't too worried about coverage for the lakes as they were already oversubscribed for matches, but I did not want to lose the fantastic investment that Dave Preston had made.

Did angling papers help?

No not really.

There were weekly reports of tiny Winter League matches, the write up often taking up half a page together with massive, exaggerated headlines, yet little more than a few column inches for the biggest league in the land, the highest Winter weights in the land, and the biggest Winter League payouts ever envisaged.

Dave Preston did not put 10 grand into my Winter Leagues for fun.

Dave was after profile for his company and all he got was a few lousy column inches that he could have bought for a hundred quid.

*****

So back to Thailand and the match that had set my juices flowing.

Here we now had a company who were putting thousands into the sport in order to raise their profile.

The internet sites had been active as had Facebook and the local media.

In little more than a month, thousands of people had become familiar with the company name, people who had never before heard of them. That is the power and the returns that sponsors can expect if they are dealing with professional people and not boy journalist.

Talking to one of the directors of the company, he was quite pleased with how the competition had helped to raise the company profile and indicated that he would like to make the competition an annual event with competitors chosen from a series of regional competitions.

Even more of a mouthwatering morsel, he told me that with the right sort of media coverage, he was prepared to invest tens of thousands into the sport.

This may appear to be a King's ransom to most of us, but for a multi-national company it represents a small proportion of their marketing budget.

Fishing does not have to rely on tackle companies for investment and sponsorship.

The countries' biggest participant sport is fully able to attract outside companies if only the NFA or whatever it is now called, and the angling media ever functioned professionally.

We all knew Micky Thill, sadly now departed.

CAPTAIN AMERICA WITH THE QUITE SUPERB ESSEX COUNTY SIDE

When he entered an American team in the Angling World Championships, he thought outside of the box, and the first sponsor that he approached came up with the goods - that company was Coca Cola, and you don't get much bigger and better than that.

CHAPTER 28

THE DUEL

There was little more than one minute to go before the starting whistle would sound.

A crowd of several hundred turned down the volume to little more than a whisper - a silent Italian whisper in anticipation of the battle to come.

Autographs had been signed, many autographs, the Italians love autographs.

The TV cameras were in place and the two protagonists turned their heads to one side, each man looking for a sign of weakness in his opponent.

The man to my left was good - he was exceptionally good, one of the best anglers in the world.

You did not become many times Italian champion without being exceptionally good, nor did you narrowly miss victory by ounces in the World Championships a couple of months earlier without being exceptionally good.

I noticed a weakness.

He had a nervous look on his face and was fidgeting.

I smiled at him.

It was a confident smile, not exactly a smirk but a smile delivered with an air of superiority that was just relaxed enough to unsettle him.

A "just another day at the office" sort of smile told him that neither his presence nor that of the TV cameras bothered me in the slightest.

In reality, I was a near nervous wreck but there was no way that I was going to allow my head-to-head opponent to see this.

Francesco Cassini was a slow starter - a nervous starter, it took him a while to settle into a rhythm.

This was his weakness - his Achilles heel.

I had to deliver a concussive blow early in the duel - a moral sapping blow - a confidence shattering blow.

How dare these upstart Italians challenge the waggler fishing authority and superiority of the English?

English pride was at stake and several million Italian TV viewers were tuned in to witness their challenge.

I desperately needed an edge.

* * * * *

I temporarily moved back in time - back to my youth - back to an important lesson in the minefield strewn education of real-life - an education that could only be taught if accompanied by occasional pain and anguish.

I was perhaps 16 years old and had been active on the Northern canal and lake circuit for almost 2 years now.

"The Boy with the Golden Arm", as the angling papers had christened me, was about to pit his youthful enthusiasm against the most seasoned of seasoned veterans.

The boy was living in the world of invincibility that invariably accompanies youth and was about to be brought down to earth by a serious kick up the rear.

Recent results had been good, and I was brimming with confidence, only today was to be the real test as to the progress made.

Little did I know that the university of life held many pitfalls, a never-ending series of painful lessons that if not taken on board would be repeated many times over.

As Einstein once said to me: "The repetition of failure coupled with the expectancy of a different result Billy, is a sure sign of madness in every match angler."

Drawn next to me on the Bridgewater canal at Grappenhall, Warrington, was one of the North's top rods - Dickie Bowker senior.

Dickie and dad had often engaged in epic fishing and psychological duels; however, I was little more than an apprentice in such worldly verbal jousts.

Now to describe Dickie without really knowing him would be difficult, suffice to say that Dickie could talk - Dickie never stopped talking yet in many ways it was for a reason.

Perhaps it would be easier to picture him if you could imagine Sir Alex Ferguson as a match fisherman.

Constant, perfectly pitched mind games travelled the airways in my direction.

Each delivery would be timed with metronomic precision - halfway through a cast - just as a bite was developing - just before or after a good fish slipped the hook.

I failed the test miserably and received the thrashing of a lifetime on a swim that was every bit as good as Dickies'.

Before the match I had always imagined that winning matches required no more than two elements - a good draw and good fishing.

I was still a kid and was to be schooled at the university of life that day by the most accomplished Professor in the business.

"Professor" Dickie Bowker had no equal and few anglers emerged unscathed after five bruising hours of continual mind games bombardment.

My dad always held up against Dickie and gave as good as he got – not so me, I was way out of my depth, totally outclassed, and buckled under the pressure of the non-stop verbal assault.

The lesson was noted and tucked away in one of the empty drawers of my youthful mind.

At the age of 16, most of the drawers in my schoolboy mind were still empty, and as life moved on, each one of them, in turn, was to be filled with a degree of knowledge, an understanding of life that was often painfully acquired through experience.

There was less than one minute to go before the duel of Palma lakes was to begin.

I searched this store of knowledge, and remembering my encounter with Dickie Bowker, the Professor; I opened the relevant drawer and dusted down the contents.

* * * * *

My mind wandered a little.

Why on earth was I the star attraction in the Champion of Champions duel?

The event had been pushed for the last few weeks on the

Italian TV sports channels as a head-to-head duel between the English champion and the Italian champion, and boisterous herds of partisan Italians were now behind us willing on their champion.

The crowd numbered literally hundreds and none of them was on my side.

Fassa, the largest Italian fishing tackle company and joint sponsors of the event, now had sole Italian distribution rights for Billy Makin floats, and for promotion purposes had arranged the event and flown me over to Italy.

At the time I held two of the three major English individual titles, the Matchman of the Year, and the BBC champion, and so they erroneously assumed that I was the English champion.

I think that Stan Piecha held the title that year, but I wasn't about to tell them.

Who was I to argue?

STAN PIECHA AND JACKIE CHARLTON

This was an all-expenses-paid jolly and the chance to promote my floats in the Italian market.

For me, it was also an ego boost.

Everyone likes to have their ego occasionally massaged, and even today I adore it when the girls in my Pattaya bar massage my ego.

No one massages egos like a Thai bar girl.

* * * * *

Francesco Casini took the lid off his bait.

The timing was everything – one minute to go.

I walked over to him.

In his bait box was the most pathetic bunch of maggots that I have ever seen. The maggots would have been ignored as inedible by an English robin.

I had worked at Alf Pendlebury's maggot farm during my school holidays in my younger days and could recognise a black fly maggot at a hundred paces.

Dickie Bowker's painfully taught lesson flashed before my eyes.

What would the old maestro have done?

How would Sir Alec Ferguson have conducted his mind games?

I needed that edge.

The man sat in front of me was special - this adversary was world-class - bloody good, probably much too good for me when on home soil.

Francesco was quite obviously nervous - he had always been a slow starter - maybe he hadn't fished in front of such large crowds before - maybe the TV camera's troubled him.

I was still outwardly composed having just finished filming a pro-celebrity series for Granada TV and a TV advert.

The cameras didn't trouble me, well, not that much.

I assumed a casual air of confident bravado coupled with indifference.

I shook my head at Francesco's bait, tut-tutted and walked back to my swim, taking out of my tackle box a 2-pint container of "Dorman's Donkeys", the biggest and best maggots in the world, bred by Terry Dorman of Nottingham.

I then walked back to Francesco and placed the container of maggots beside him. "For you", I said.

DORMAN'S DONKEYS

His jaw dropped.

I read his mind.

Who the hell was this cocky little bounder who was now in a head-to-head duel with him in front of a TV audience of millions?

How could he possibly hand over half of his bait if he were not supremely confident of success?

Just how good did this bloody Englishman think that he was?

I saw the doubt, both in his eyes and in his demeanour as his confidence drained away.

He was visibly wilting before my eyes.

I witnessed an almost imperceptible tremble as he lovingly caressed the finest maggots ever seen in Italy, a look of disbelief momentarily flickering across his face.

He tried to disguise it, but he was too late, "Professor" Bowker had struck a mortally wounding blow, exactly as he had done to me all those years before.

I returned to my swim as the whistle sounded for what was to become an exciting and intriguing game of cat and mouse, every move cheered by several hundred Italians and watched by millions.

"Thank you, Dickie Bowker, you old rascal", I whispered under my breath as my peacock waggler sailed serenely towards the island in Parma Lake.

THE ISLAND IN PARMA LAKE

We were both casting to the island, and a couple of yards to the left of Francesco was a large, overhanging willow tree.

Maybe this was a slight advantage to Francesco, but it was a tricky cast and required precision and concentration.

I had gained an important psychological advantage.

Francesco was nervous, and definitely unsettled by the bait I had given him seconds before the starting whistle - I wasn't finished there.

My mind once again flashed back to the exact moment when as a cocky young teenager I had been on the receiving end of psychological warfare by Dickie Bowker, the old master of mind games.

My waggler flew straight and true to the Island; halfway through Francesco's back cast, I shouted "Good Luck Francesco", exactly as Dickie had done to me all those years before.

The result was predictably the same.

That day my waggler had disappeared into a bed of brambles on the Bridgewater canal, and now, with his concentration broken, Francesco's waggler buried itself deep into the willow tree resulting in a break above the float.

The crowd groaned.

"Thank you, Dickie,", I whispered under my breath.

Looking back on it, I now guiltily realize that this was gamesmanship, little different to a professional foul, but at the time my mindset was considerably more serious than the more mellow approach to life brought on by age and the sense of fair play.

My float disappeared and a carp like creature called a Carassius of a pound or so was soon in the net.

CARASSIUS

This was followed by several more before Francesco managed to re-tackle and give chase.

Things went badly for him for the next half hour, as playing "catch up" is always difficult and leads to an unconscious need to speed things up; this inevitably results in bad timing and missed bites.

For the TV coverage, the duel was little more than a two-and-a-half-hour sprint, and by the one-hour mark, I guess that I would be some 10 pounds in the lead.

Every fish that I caught was greeted with polite applause - every fish caught by Francesco resulted in loud, raucous cheers.

Some two hours into the duel and the cheers were becoming more and more frequent, the applause less so.

Francesco was narrowing the gap and steadily making inroads into my lead. Perhaps the overhanging willow tree was giving him an advantage - perhaps local knowledge was beginning to come into play. Either way, the crowd could sense that their champion had not only closed the gap but was possibly in the lead and flying to an almost certain victory.

The strangest thing now happened.

A kid of about 10 years old clambered under the rope that kept the crowd back and handed me his autograph book and a pen.

As I was between casts, I signed his book, whereupon he then gave me a couple of slices of bread.

Did the little blighter know something that I didn't?

His dad called him over, so I turned around and gestured that it was OK for the kid to sit with me.

Pinching on a piece of flake I cast over to the island, and within five minutes I was slipping the net under a 3lb carp.

Up to this point, neither of us had caught a carp, Carassius being the only fish in our nets.

Francesco and I were now pretty much on level terms.

The anticipation in the crowd was growing and reaching near fever pitch.

Francesca netted a couple of quick Carassius, the crowd cheered, and once again we were neck and neck as a 2lb carp grabbed my bread flake; the crowd groaned.

Excitable creatures the Italians.

I recast, again with a pinch of bread on the hook, and once again the float disappeared - I struck, and something solid swam directly towards me.

What I did next still baffles me to this day; I sat the kid on my tackle box and handed him the rod.

This was more than a head-to-head duel; it was a promotional exercise for both Fassa and Billy Makin floats and the crowd loved the gesture.

The TV camera's moved closer, ignoring Francesco and focusing on the kid; the crowd went quiet as he quite expertly played the fish, the odd word of encouragement being shouted by the crowd, me occasionally reaching over to adjust the clutch for him, and soon I slid the net under a 5-pound carp.

The crowd went wild, cheering and clapping loud enough to be heard all over Parma.

Francesco was quietly observing proceedings and probably wondering what I would do next.

I unhooked the carp and shouted over to Francesco; he watched open-mouthed, as, with a theatrical flourish, I threw the fish back into the lake instead of my keepnet.

He visibly wilted.

Just how confident was this bloody Englishman who could treat the duel of Parma lakes - the Champion of Champion's event in such a cavalier fashion?

He recast - his confidence wavering, and once again his waggler disappeared deep into the willow tree.

I now had a good five minutes to re-establish my lead before he could set up again, and with a little over 10 minutes left, I now held the advantage.

"Thank you, Dickie Bowker", I again whispered under my breath.

The country's honour was back on track.

Two more good sized carp took the bread flake; they did go into my net, and a final flourish of Carassius by Francesco produced a nail-biting finish that sent the crowd into a frenzy.

Little more than a few ounces separated us at the scales.

* * * * *

I have to say the Italians have a completely different approach to their sportsmen than the English do.

As a guest, I was treated like royalty from the moment that I first approached Parma lakes, and passing the rod to the kid immediately split the crowd's allegiance down the middle.

The last few frenzied minutes of the match climaxed with half the crowd cheering me on and the other half cheering Francesco's every move.

The event had also been sponsored by an Italian wine company, and soon gallons of the stuff was swilling around, much of it down my gullet.

The hospitality was overwhelming and to soak up the wine half a cow was barbecued at Palma's finest restaurant for the benefit of Francesco and myself.

It would be some 3 or 4 days later that the fax from Fassa arrived at my float factory.

I almost choked when I saw the size of the order.

The head-to-head duel had been shown live on the Italian sports channel and it seemed that suddenly everyone in Italy wanted Billy Makin peacock wagglers.

Within minutes I was on the phone with Mr Surana of New Delhi, India.

"How many thousands of full peacock feathers did you say Mr Bolly?" he said in disbelief.

It had been a good week all round.

Fish, champagne, a whole new set of friends and memories that will never fade.

CHAPTER 29

BLACKMAIL – WHO ME?

Several years ago, when knights still jousted on horseback, I was involved in the fishing tackle trade as a float maker.

Now in those days, the trade was largely controlled by 3 or 4 big wholesalers who by virtue of their insistence on obtaining "exclusives" on brand names from the manufacturers, pretty much had the power of life or death over them.

In simple terms, if you only sell to ONE wholesaler and he drops your product, you are out of business.

My wholesaler at the time was the biggest in the country and was owned by someone who when I first met him appeared to be a pompous upper-class twit.

As time passed, I discovered that he was in fact a pompous upper-class twit and being fully aware of the strangle hold that he had over us manufacturers, continued to act like a pompous upper-class twit at every opportunity.

I had to make contingency plans to lessen his power over my company and ultimately get rid of him, but how?

The answer of course was - cunningly.

Keeping things pretty much hush, hush, I moved into the "Vanman" market during the winter months when things were quiet and set up a completely different distribution system.

Now the "Vanman" was nothing more than a man with a large van which was decked out with shelves, these, in turn, being full of the smaller items of fishing tackle plus an assortment of redundant items that the manufacturers wanted to offload cheaply. These guys were essential for thinning out old or discontinued product lines that the major wholesalers wouldn't touch with a barge pole.

Acting very much in a "Del Boy" capacity, the Vanman then drove round to the individual tackle shops and topped up anything that was running short, thereby saving the tackle shop owner from having to wait around for the big wholesalers to deliver by post or carrier.

You may recognize the name of my first "Vanman" wholesaler, the company being called Wovencrest, run by a couple of conmen known as Colin Perry and John Dean.

During the winter months, I quietly expanded the stable of Vanmen to six, so that I now had some leverage when the pompous upper-class twit wanted to begin telling me what I had to produce for the coming season, how much discount he wanted, and when he was going to pay.

Naturally enough, there was major conflict and trauma when I had my Spring meeting with the wholesale company, only now it was me who dictated the terms of trading to the "well-bred man", rather than sitting quietly like a terrified schoolboy in the headmaster's office as he brandished the cane.

At times during the meeting, he appeared to be on the verge of exploding and constantly threatened that the fires of hell would be my future.

He was in reality totally b-----sed, as I had held off the meeting until his spanking new glossy catalogue had been printed in the thousands, with Billy Makin floats featuring prominently, plastered across four pages in full colour.

We naturally enough parted company the following year, by which time I had established enough outlets to more than cover for the loss of the country's biggest wholesaler, despite the issued threats of a well-bred, pompous, upper- class twit.

Having finally broken free of the strangle hold of the big four wholesalers, it was now time to begin the export drive of Billy Makin floats.

The timing was perfect.

England had finally arrived on the world stage, and a series of individual and team wins in the world championships had not gone unnoticed by the continentals.

Most of the early England success had been achieved by waggler fishing, while the main continental sides had been fishing poles. This left them severely limited on range and ensured that the English long-range tactics were pretty much unchallenged.

And so it was that the next three years found me in Florence at the AIPO international angling show, not exhibiting, more a case of making contacts among some of Europe's biggest wholesalers and manufacturers.

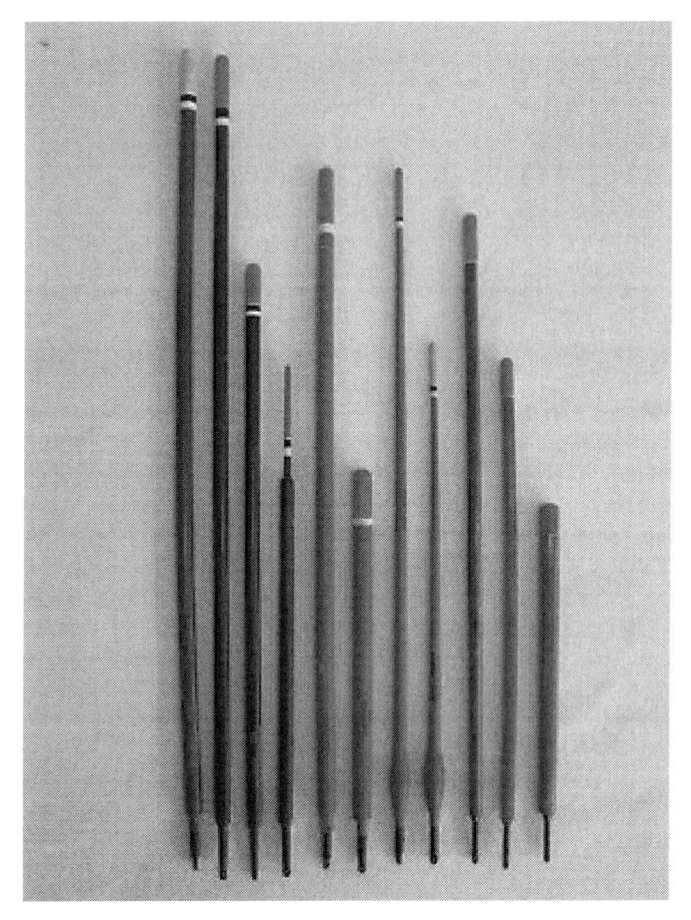

A SELECTION OF MY WAGGLERS BOUGHT BY FASSA

At this point, I have to apologize for the timing and sequencing of the events, but in the midst of time, thanks to a combination of some pretty raucous evenings in Florence and a 30 plus year gap, many of the stories have become intertwined.

One evening found me at one of Florence's top restaurants, where the owner of one of Italy's top angling companies (Fassa) was playing host accompanied by Mario Molinari, a name I am sure many English matchmen are familiar with.

MARIO MOLINARI

As the boss man spoke no English, Mario acted as interpreter, and Italian wine by the bucketful flowed freely, so much so that the English contingent had quite happily forgiven the Italians for siding with Hitler.

As Fassa had now taken on my floats and were the exclusive distributers of Daiwa tackle in Italy, John Middleton, the Daiwa boss and myself were pretty much guests of honour and were sat either side of the boss man; everyone getting more and more drunk as the evening went on.

He leaned over to Mario and spoke - Mario translated and told me that the boss man, who was a respected wine connoisseur and extremely rich, wanted to know what I thought of his choice in wine and Italian wines in general?

I felt a little Michael taking coming on.

"Very nice," I told Mario. "Almost as good as the French wines."

Mario translated.

The boss man's eyes opened wide.

He snapped his fingers, and a waiter came running.

Words were exchanged, and a couple of minutes later a rather expensive bottle appeared, the boss man himself pouring the contents into a brand-new glass which he swirled around before handing it to me.

All eyes around the table were now focused on me.

I had suddenly become a wine connoisseur and the room went quiet.

I sniffed the wine, gently and expertly swilling it as I did so; I then took a long gulp and smiled in appreciation.

The boss man appeared satisfied and spoke to Mario.

"Better than French wines?" Mario asked.

"Delicious," I replied. "Very few French wines are better than this."

Mario translated.

The boss man's eyes almost popped out of his head, as once again he snapped his fingers and the waiter came running before disappearing down into the bowels of the restaurant's cellar, reappearing cradling a bottle of rare Italian wine worth several hundred pounds, several years old, and covered in dust.

I had pushed my luck as far as it could go by now, and after tasting, pronounced that Italian wines were indeed the best in the world; John and I then proceeded to down several glasses of the vintage Italian plonk before anyone else at the table could get a sniff in.

Still, the boss man willingly paid the bill, and later in the evening walked away quite happily content in the knowledge that one of England's finest wine aficionadas had given his seal of approval to Italian wines.

How was the wine?

Well, John and I desperately needed a pint, and so off we wandered to the Riverside nightclub alongside the fish-filled River Arno.

* * * * *

On entering the club, we were now accompanied by Roberto Trabucco, a man who always reminded me of the Peter Sellers' version of a Mafioso.

THE GODFATHER – ROBERTO TRABUCCO

Roberto appeared to be a regular at the place and received immediate personal attention as we were escorted by an extremely nervous waiter type chap to the best seats in the house.

I couldn't help feeling that we were in the company of Don Corleone from the Godfather.

Maybe I was right about Roberto, after all, he did make pretty good pole floats.

Inside, all six of us, now pretty well sozzled after the gallons of red wine sat down and ordered drinks.

Roberto, the Godfather clicked his fingers.

Within seconds, we were surrounded by a group of very pretty, lightly clad girl hostesses, all of whom were of Eastern European extraction.

David Bird, who was at the show representing the NFA, and quite wobbly and merry thanks to the wine consumed at the restaurant, began entertaining a couple of the girls by buying them pots of tea, (I kid you not) all on his NFA charge card, each pot costing in the region of thirty quid.

This was over thirty years ago so you can imagine what it would cost now.

We managed to get rid of the girls until an absolutely drop-dead gorgeous blond Bulgarian film star ambled up and sat between John Middleton and myself, her legs stretching halfway across the club.

I bought her a drink.

John bought her a drink.

Then the bill for the 2 drinks arrived.

"Clucking bells," I said.

She got no more drinks and soon disappeared, meanwhile, David continued buying pots of tea for the girls, ordered in his quintessentially English voice that only ever seemed to surface after many drinks.

* * * * *

I suppose that it would be some 3 years later as I was putting the finishing touches to Lake 1, on Phase 1 of Makin Fisheries, that I bumped into John and his wife Rosie working his Daiwa stand at the National Angling Show at the NEC.

JOHN MIDDLETON – DAIWA BOSS

"I'm looking for a sponsor for my lakes," I explained, going on to tell him of my plan to make the complex into the first commercial fishery in Europe, and with an angler capacity of several hundred.

John wasn't too impressed and exhibited the same sort of indifference that I was now finding wherever I turned.

The whole idea was a little crazy and would never work, everyone told me so.

We took a little walk to the bar.

"It will work." I persisted. "Anglers will jump at the chance of catching lots of fish in secure surroundings. There will be toilets and food on site. When you return to your car it will still have four wheels on the outside and a radio on the inside. You won't have to walk miles and will not need wellies or waders. There will be no boats, no dogshit, no floods."

"Sorry Billy, I've used up all my marketing budget for the year," he went on. "Once it is up and running, come back and see me next year."

I suddenly had a cunning plan.

"Great time down the Riverside club in Florence that night John, did you ever mention to Rosie about that gorgeous Bulgarian girl with the legs?"

"Bulgarian girl? - Legs?"

"Don't you remember John?"

"No, I was pretty drunk that night, I can't remember a thing after we left the restaurant."

"Oh dear, how sad, never mind," I said in my best Windsor Davis voice. "So you never mentioned the Bulgarian girl to Rosie then?"

John Middleton went quiet for a minute or so as he mentally dissolved deep into troubled thoughts before my eyes.

I held my breath, hoping that his mind was indeed a blank.

"I suppose that DAIWA MAKIN FISHERIES does have a certain ring to it." He said. "How much is it going to cost me, Makin, you scheming, conniving, little 'bounder'?"

And so it came to pass that the embryonic Makin Fisheries became Daiwa Makin Fisheries, a fruitful association that lasted for many years.

Dick Clegg joined us at the table.

Dick had been with us all that night in Florence.

I wondered.

Just how much did Sir Richard remember about the evening?

Now then, what could the England team manager possibly do for me?

CLEGGY – THE GREATEST TEAM MANAGER OF THEM ALL

I smiled at the thought; I was not a team man and had already turned Stan Smith down a few years earlier.

On reflection, I suppose that the darned expensive investment in the leggy Bulgarian girl turned out (quite innocently of course) to be one of my more inspired business moves.

CHAPTER 30

DAVE

Perhaps something that modern-day anglers are not aware of is the cyclical nature of fishing, many of them having spent most of their time on commercials.

Now by cyclical, I am not referring to methods of fishing or the obvious advances in fishing tackle; I am pointing the finger at the fish themselves.

* * * * *

It was Saturday the 30th of July 1966, as dad and I sat on the Bridgewater canal at Grappenhall fishing for perch. By my side was a little transistor radio and the English football team were in the process of winning the world cup.

The air was still and an eerie quiet descended across the country; no tractors were working the fields and no cars were on the roads.

The whole country had ground to a halt in anticipation of England's first-ever world cup triumph.

Two obvious questions arise.

Why were we the only people on the entire length of the Bridgey, and why were we fishing for perch when for the last few years every match had been won with either roach or bream.

The answer to the first part is quite obvious, nothing came before fishing; the second though is a little more complex.

The previous season had seen Dad and I sit for 4 hours on the same canal on June 16th, the fishing season opening day, fishing for non-existent roach. A mystery virus known as Columnaris had devastated roach stocks throughout the country during the closed season, and almost every Stillwater had become virtually fishless.

Nature abhors a vacuum, and the ever opportunist perch bred with gay abandum to fill that vacuum, resulting in a canal that was solid with perch, with just an odd bream shoal and precious little else.

For several years, matchmen were forced to target perch and nothing else, and those that cracked the technique began to win regularly.

Over the years, the roach gradually came back and along came a different virus that the angling press named Perchitis and perch disappeared countrywide.

Judging from some of the match reports that I see on Facebook, there appears to be a massive increase in the perch and skimmer population in commercials and throughout the country's canals at the moment, and both species are becoming the main target for many matchmen.

Now along with the cyclical changes in fish populations, there have been several changes in diet, in modern times the most obvious one being from luncheon meat and sweetcorn to the pellet. There was however a period during the beginning of the '80s when for some strange reason, every roach in the country decided that under no circumstances were they ever going to eat a caster again.

I kid you not about this; there were actually waters that were solid with roach where you could literally dangle a caster for 5 hours without so much as a bite.

* * * * *

The starting whistle sounded and my bodied peacock waggler flew perfectly across the North bank of the Nene, cocked immediately, and within seconds settled as the bulk shot reached a point some 3ft from the bottom, to be followed by a final setting as the two number 6 shot came into play.

It should be noted that the bodied peacock float was already loaded, this being essential when slider fishing, as without this loading the float slides up the line to the stop knot during the cast and range is much reduced.

Three soft balls of caster filled groundbait followed, not all at the float, but each one a couple of yards or so downstream, giving a line of feed for the float to travel along with the slight flow.

The single caster tripped slowly along the bottom in textbook fashion, the way it had always done on the North bank under such perfect conditions. It was just a matter of time before the inevitable happened and the action would begin.

Poor Dave Thomas (A former World Champion) on the next peg downstream sprayed a pouchful of those disgusting bronze maggots in front of him and cast out his small waggler.

DAVE WITH HIS WORLD CHAMPIONSHIP WINNING CATCH

I almost felt sorry for him.

This was the North bank for God's sake.

To treat such an esteemed match fishery with this level of contempt was tantamount to sacrilege, and although a prison sentence was perhaps a little harsh, a severe reprimand and a good birching would most certainly have been in order.

I wound in, re-baited, and recast, secure in the knowledge that very soon, a succession of prime roach, followed a few bonus skimmers would be finding sanctuary in my keepnet.

Dave slipped his landing net under a half-pound roach.

"Even a blind squirrel bumps into an occasional acorn," I thought, and waited expectantly for the orange-tipped slider to disappear as it travelled serenely through the swim.

We were now one hour into the match.

Something was wrong - something was very wrong.

I still hadn't registered a single bite and Dave was now well into his stride, with roach after roach being either swung to hand or netted.

I studied Dave's approach.

He was terrible.

Instead of grouping his maggots, he was spraying them over half a tennis court.

His casting was all over the place. He couldn't drop his waggler within 2 or 3 yards of his previous cast, yet still, the roach kept coming.

I have in fact mentioned something similar in a previous chapter, where Mark Pollard won a match next peg to me fishing equally atrociously on the squatt.

Still bite less after 2 hours, I saw Dave switch to his stick float rig as the fish had now moved in closer.

Instead of tightening things up as I would have expected, nothing changed. He was possibly even worse than he had been on the waggler.

Instead of feeding with his catapult, he was now throwing in those disgusting bronze maggots' over-arm, again spreading them over half a tennis court.

His casting was equally bad.

His stick float would land 3 yards downstream one cast, and the next cast it would be 3 yards farther out.

The roach kept coming.

How on earth had this man achieved such a level of dominance on the Trent?

Half of the world's supply of money-filled brown envelopes had already travelled North to his Leeds' home during the early part of the season, a repeat of the previous season I have to add.

He couldn't fish!

He could neither feed nor cast accurately.

He was hopeless.

Then again, maybe I wasn't seeing the full picture.

Dave slipped his landing net under yet another prime roach.

At the weigh-in, Dave's match-winning catch took the scales round to near 15lb, ounces in front of an equally bad angler known as John Dean, who had fished a similar method.

I never had one single bite on the caster throughout the match.

It was a chastened me that stayed awake that night waiting for the penny to drop.

Both Dave and John knew exactly what they were doing.

Neither angler wanted the fish shoaled in a tight area; they wanted them chasing, competing, and scattered over an area big enough not to be spooked as a procession of their mates disappeared.

This was exactly the same approach that Polly (Mark Pollard) adopted with his squatt fishing.

It was something that I could never really get my head around – splitting a shoal of fish was anathema to me; my fishing approach had always been to bunch the fish in as tight an area as possible, yet on reflection, my masterclass lesson that fateful day at Attenborough Gravels with Ivan Marks had warned against such an approach.

CHAPTER 31

BORIS

It's a funny old thing the human brain.

There are times when it can be pretty darn useful, and times when it makes decisions on its own without your being aware of it.

Generally speaking, I have a pretty good memory, sometimes approaching total recall, of much of my life's fishing exploits, and when focusing on one particular match, even one of over 50 years ago, I seem to have the ability to transport myself back in time and relive the experience as if it were yesterday.

Sometimes, however, if you are going through a particularly traumatic period in life, the brain can erase virtually all memories of that period as a form of a defence mechanism, and whole episodes in life come up with a big fat blank when trying to recall events of that period.

And so it is that I can now only just transport myself to a team meeting for what I think was possibly an important event on the Trent.

Maybe it was with the Coleshill National side or maybe it was with Coventry, I honestly can't remember, nor can I remember fishing the match in question.

I was going through a messy, one-sided divorce, and virtually 2 years of my life seemed to be on hold; my brain having decided to protect me by simply erasing vast tracts of that life during the entire period.

* * * * *

I was at a team meeting, so I must have been in a bad way as I hated team meetings even more than I disliked team fishing.

At the front of the class was the imposing psychotic figure of the tyrannical headmaster himself – a giant of a man who went under the pseudonym of BORIS – real name Frank Barlow.

This headmaster didn't need a cane to bring the class to order, one glance could stop a steam train dead in its tracks.

THE UNFORGETTABLE FRANK BARLOW

It had been several years since my equally traumatic experience at the hands of Dave Thomas that day on the North bank of the Nene, sadly, no matter how hard I tried, this was one experience where the brain and I conflicted, as it stubbornly refused to erase one single second of the match.

I had bitten the bullet and forsaken my beloved casters.

I was now a part of the spray, pray, and be damned brigade, returning home after every match looking like I had just been Tango'd, scraping and scrubbing my fluorescent orange and yellow Chrysodine stained hands in the hope that whatever female victim succumbed to my Brad Pitt like charms that evening wouldn't insist on my wearing boxing gloves as we tried to keep warm under the bed clothes.

Over the past few weeks, I had noticed an unusually high number of chub being caught on the Trent.

Surely chub preferred casters to those disgusting bronze maggots, and so I decided to put it to the test with a day's pleasure fishing at Long Eaton, where I alternated between caster and bronze maggot, and indeed, so it proved - we had come almost full circle.

The chub definitely preferred casters and the roach bronze maggots.

Armed with 3 pints of proper bait, I came second with 29lb of chub at Clifton on the following Saturday afternoon, being probably the only angler in the entire match fishing the caster and resolved to tell the team members that evening at the stupid weekly team meeting.

The team had asked the headmaster, Frank Barlow, to come along and give a talk on how they should approach the coming National Championships, and naturally enough, the entire talk centred around the bronze maggot.

"What about the caster Frank?" I asked.

Boris Barlow fixed me with an intimidating stare.

"Don't even think about it Billy," he roared. "No one must even think about taking one single caster to the match. This is a bronze maggot only match, and to have any chance of beating the Trentmen, bronze maggots are ALL you will take."

I decided not to mention my second place on the caster that very afternoon - the headmaster was still glaring menacingly at me.

*****

It was now one week after the team meeting and what had appeared as a veiled threat from one of the Trent's finest anglers.

You argued with big Frank Barlow at your peril, yet here I was, sitting on a perfect Trent swim on a perfect stick float day, armed with 4 pints of casters left over from a big-money invitation match on the private bank at Coombe Abbey on the previous Wednesday.

I had 4 pints of bronze maggots as back up, but the 29lb of chub that I had caught the previous week had convinced me that things were coming around full circle, and once again there was a place for the caster.

The whistle sounded, and close on 200 anglers each fired either a handful or a pouchful of bronze maggots into the river, and one solitary fool slipped a caster onto his hook, swung out his stick float, and followed up with a dozen casters.

The black-tipped wire stem stick sailed serenely down the 4ft deep swim.

This was angling perfection.

This was the sort of swim and the sort of day where the planets had surely aligned, and even 5 hours without a bite would not have been a problem.

Nothing in life could have been better.

I didn't need 72 virgins in paradise.

All I needed was 4 pints of casters, a wire stem stick, and a smooth flowing, fish-filled swim on the Trent.

Little did I know that this was the day that I was to enter paradise.

* * * * *

My mind moved back in time to the previous week.

It had been a difficult match and the 29lb of chub had seriously flattered me. On a different day it could have so easily been 40lb.

The swim had been a little too shallow, and the slight breeze had been in my face, resulting in endless tangles and an amateurish attempt at line control.

If only I had switched to the waggler sooner.

The chub had been queueing up to feed, yet good anglers all

around me had struggled on their bronze maggots.

Was my swim so much better than theirs or was it the bait?

* * * * *

I was still in fantasy mode as the float disappeared.

Darn it, I didn't even strike, I was still re-living the previous week's match.

I returned to the present, re-baited, re-cast, and watched almost mesmerised as the stick settled to the shot and moved slowly downstream, travelling in perfect alignment with both my mind and the river.

Some halfway down the swim it sank and a 2oz chub came to hand.

I checked its mouth; a tip Dave Thomas had given me a couple of years earlier.

If it was full of bait, I was feeding too much.

Its mouth was empty, so the swim had a few fish in it.

I upped the feeding, and the next swim down saw a 1lb chub slip into my keepnet.

The next four hours passed in the blink of an eye.

Chub after chub grabbed the caster.

I didn't even need to control the stick - they were now directly in front of me and were taking the caster on the drop.

At virtually the 4-hour mark, I run out of casters and switched to the bronze maggot.

The fish didn't disappear, but for the last hour I caught no more than half a dozen much smaller fish.

* * * * *

That evening, I skipped the team meeting as I had a date with a pretty little brunette who was eager to learn about my technique with the waggler.

Once again Frank was holding court, and once again he was impressing upon everyone the need to take bronze maggots and nothing else.

One chap who had been present at the match that day interrupted.

"What about the caster Frank?"

"Forget the blessed caster." Frank almost shouted in frustration. "Don't listen to that idiot Makin, the caster no longer works on the Trent. How many times do I have to tell you?"

"Haven't you heard Frank?"

"Heard what?"

"Billy broke the Trent match record this afternoon with 54lb on the stick float and caster."

"WHAT?" Boris Barlow exploded. "Wait till I get my hands on the little "bounder", he did that just to make me look stupid."

Perhaps it was as well that I stayed away from that night's team meeting, besides, I was much too busy demonstrating my waggler technique with my little brunette.

The planets had indeed aligned that day.

CHAPTER 32

THE BUBBLE

T'was around 12 years ago.

I had just arrived back in England from my home in Tenerife on my way to see my mum in the nursing home in Lancashire, and being unable to get a flight to Manchester, I had flown into Birmingham and picked up a hire car.

The radio told me that as usual the M6 was blocked, and so I took the old country road that I had travelled along so many times and so many years earlier with dad in his 3 wheeled Reliant.

My heart missed a beat at the road sign.

SANDON.

Oh my God, I had to stop; memories of times long forgotten began to surface. Visions of men long gone - men who in their time were revered - men who were heroes of mine as I grew up among the Lancashire coal mines and cotton mills. These were men who I had spent countless hours watching, observing, and gathering up years of their experience and knowledge as they went about their business. I was little more than a sponge, excitedly absorbing every morsel of fishing information offered. These men had kept no secrets - they were men who quite liked the fact that a young pretender had arrived to challenge the old order.

I took a left and travelled the 300 yards to the canal bridge.

My palms were sweating in anticipation as I left the hire car.

I was 16 again - a kid - and just below the bridge was the most famous swim in Britain - THE BUBBLE.

THE BUBBLE

No one knew where the water from the bubble came from, it was simply a large volume of water that flushed into the canal below Sandon lock, and more importantly, it was always pegged number 250.

Peg 250 was an aquarium, and to win a Stoke City match you had to beat the man who drew peg 250 - it was as simple as that.

There was only one snag.

Peg 250 never seemed to be in the draw bag - everyone knew

that.

It was rumoured throughout the match fishing grapevine that the Stoke City matches were a little suspect to say the least.

Two weeks before the Staffordshire Championship, fishing the bread punch, I had taken second place in a 500 pegger; needless to say the bubble peg had more than doubled my weight.

I walked down the two-hundred-year-old worn stone steps and under the bridge to THE BUBBLE swim, wondering how many thousands of horses had passed beneath that very bridge towing their barges laden with goods on their way to who knows where.

There had been no motorways and no cars in 1777 when the 93-mile-long Trent and Mersey canal had been completed, and before the coming of the age of steam and the railways, canals had formed their own super-highways as they criss-crossed the country.

I moved on some 5 yards below the gushing water and looked down at the ground.

Were those slight circular indentations in the ground where my wicker basket had sat over 40 years earlier?

My eyes misted over as the memories came flooding back.

Did I really draw the bubble in the Staffordshire Championships?

No.

I couldn't have; it had to be my mind playing tricks on me.

Peg 250 was reserved for "friends" of the secretary, everyone knew that.

*****

Ghosts from the past again appeared as the hypnotic effect of the swirling water mesmerised me.

Ghosts whose faces were as clear as they had been when, as a kid, I had pestered them to death for a handful of casters, maybe even a float.

Benny Ashurst, Billy Hughes, Ginger Pennington.

Men long gone, yet magically, in my mind's eye, they were there, sitting in the bubble peg as if time had never moved on, casting either their stick floats or wagglers into the swirling cauldron of fish soup.

They had all drawn the famous bubble peg over the years.

One year, almost the entire Stoke City national winning side had mysteriously drawn the swims down from the bubble the day after their Trent triumph.

*****

My eyes returned to the 4 indentations in the ground.

There were 750 anglers taking part this day, and 3 swims down from the bubble was Tony Knight, one of the famous Abbey Hey quartet that was monopolising the Trent circuit with their stick float and caster techniques. Tony Bielderman, Ian Allcock, and a chap called Ian Heaps made up the rest of the money collection team.

COULD IAN HAVE BEEN THE GREATEST OF THEM ALL?

Ian was there with his dad, Jim, a good friend of my dad and was to become World Champion in the not-too-distant future.

Tony was on a roll, and at the time was winning everything in sight.

Tony was perhaps the favourite on the day, followed by the

association secretary, who had amazingly drawn the noted bream swim close to his cottage.

He knew the swim well and had been fishing it all week.

I lowered my head and looked down more closely.

There were definitely four holes in the ground. Small round holes, too close together to be made by the legs of a normal wicker fishing basket. Mine had been a small one.

Maybe - just maybe, they could well have been all of 40 years old.

I closed my eyes, and as I entered my time machine, found myself back in the village hall in Weston a couple of miles further down the canal at exactly the moment that my hand plunged deep into the draw bag.

* * * * *

At this point I have to explain a little of how Matchfishing worked during the '60s.

Unlike today's 'named draw', you bought a ticket, paid your pools money, handed over the ticket to the man with the bag and drew out a number.

At no time was your name and number recorded.

You simply produced the drawn peg card to the scales man at the weigh-in.

Naturally, this left the system wide open to cheating and not only could you swap pegs with a friend, but you could also buy several tickets and therefore draw several pegs, as with so many competitors there could be up to half a dozen bags, each one containing over a hundred numbers.

* * * * *

Would my rumoured Golden Arm still perform in a match of this size?

As my hand stirred the contents, one particular piece of folded cardboard seemed to stick.

It just seemed to feel right.

My fingers tingled.

Was this fate or simply serendipity?

Somehow, I just knew that it was a little special - maybe even the key to my first ever major title.

Only the Birmingham BIG-UN and certain river championships had more than the 750 anglers of the Staffordshire Championship on the Midlands match circuit.

My mouth opened wide as I opened the folded peg number.

"Come on Billy," Dad said, standing behind me. "Hurry up."

I didn't move - I couldn't.

My eyes opened wide in disbelief.

My hands began to tremble.

A bead of sweat ran down my forehead; gravity helping it along my nose and onto the floor of the old village hall.

"Bloody hell," I said.

Normally, swearing in front of dad would have resulted in a slap around the ear hole.

"Bloody hell." Said dad, as he glanced at the draw ticket.

"Bloody hell." Said the Stoke City angling official who was holding the draw bag. "What was that doing in there?"

In my 16-year-old hand was peg number 250 - THE BUBBLE, and it certainly wasn't going back into the draw bag.

* * * * *

I once again glanced down at the indentations in the ground, 3 yards below the bubble, 40 years later.

That was certainly where I had sat.

They seemed to be the right size and were definitely in the right place.

The water was still swirling at my feet as it had done all those years before, and the gentle slack, flanked by overhanging brambles on the far side simply screamed out fish.

Deja Vue overwhelmed me - my eyes misted over as I again visualised anglers long gone who had sat there before and after me.

How many had legally drawn THE BUBBLE and how many had simply been handed it?

Were the offspring of those bream and roach I had caught still swimming around in the aquarium I wondered?

Was Tony Knight's 4lb chub still living 2 swims below me?

Were the bream shoals still to be found behind the association secretary's cottage?

* * * * *

It was to be well over 20 years after my encounter with the bubble that I again fished the Staffordshire Championships.

The venue had been changed to Norbury Junction and the entry was now reduced to 180.

As I was handed the trophy, I could barely hold back the tears as I looked at the names of all those long-departed anglers inscribed into the brass plate.

There was mine, sandwiched between two of the greatest anglers of their generation, and my mind couldn't help returning to the bubble.

I remembered an age where matches with less than a hundred anglers competing were referred to as sweepstakes and barely made the local press.

An age where fibreglass was beginning to replace cane and tubular steel rods and to have acquired a Mitchell reel carried more prestige than owning a car.

This wasn't the beginning of the golden age of match fishing, but it was pretty darn close.

I guess that it evolved slowly during the post-war years and began to gather momentum during the sixties as better transport and slightly increased wealth came along.

As I again looked across at the BUBBLE PEG, a fin cut through the water and seemed to wave at me.

I grinned and waved back as I said out loud. "Thank you for the memories."

* * * * *

My second victory in the Staffordshire Championship brought a close to my Matchfishing career.

My Golden Arm at the draw bag had decided to put in one final appearance weeks before I officially retired from competition.

It had been one heck of a ride.

CHAPTER 33

AND FINALLY

As the book has been compiled from the articles that I wrote for various fishing magazines, there are many omissions of "Great Anglers", the main reason being that generally speaking, most people prefer a certain match circuit, usually a local one, and only occasionally did I come into contact with them.

How could I possibly miss one of the greatest anglers of them all?

I am of course referring to Alan Scotthorne, a man who unbelievably won the individual World Championship on 5 occasions.

The last time that I saw Alan was down my lakes, (Makin Fisheries) when he was practising for the UK Championships.

Stuck on his tackle box was a fishery sticker which meant that he had paid the 5 quid day ticket.

"I'm sorry that you paid Alan," I said. "There is a fishery policy that all England Internationals fish for free."

"That's good of you Billy." He said as he pushed out 14 meters of pole to the far banking. "Does that mean I can have my 5 quid back then Billy?"

"Love to Al," I replied. "Unfortunately, there is also a fishery policy of no refunds."

I walked off with a big grin on my face; I will leave you to guess Alan's response.

ALAN SCOTTHORNE – 5 TIMES WORLD CHAMPION

Snapping at Alan's heels among the all-time greats is Bob Nudd, 4 times world champion.

Along with Alan and Bob, I also must mention both Tommy Pickering and Denis White, and how dare I miss out Dick Clegg, probably the finest team manager of them all.

ANOTHER NATIONAL VICTORY FOR THE BARNSLEY BLACKS

Pushing Dick hard for the above accolade would most certainly be Clive Smith, the former Birmingham team captain, and Mark Downes of the Starlets, who like Dick became an England team manager.

THE GREAT CLIVE SMITH

Individually, English anglers have won far more than their fair share of world titles.

BOB NUDD HOLDS THE TEAM WORLD CLUB TROPHY WITH ESSEX COUNTY

The great Billy Lane started the ball rolling, followed by Robin Harris and then Ian Heaps. The list goes on – Kev - Dave – another Dave – Tommy – Will – Clive.

CLIVE BRANSON – WELSH WORLD CHAMPION

DAVE ROPER – WORLD CHAMPION

WILL RAISON – WORLD CHAMPION, WITH STEVIE GARDNER

ROBIN HARRIS – WORLD CHAMPION

Perhaps there are more modern icons lining up to fill the gaps left by the anglers from the GOLDEN AGE OF MATCH FISHING, but the passing of each one of them leaves a void that will take a lot of filling.

I am proud to have been both around and involved in

THE GOLDEN YEARS

THESE WERE MY MEMORIES

Billy

WOULD YOU PLEASE CONSIDER LEAVING A REVIEW?

Just a few short words would help others decide
if this memoir is for them.

Visit www.amazon.com and your "Orders" page where
you can leave your comments and thoughts.

Best regards and thanks in advance.
Billy Makin

◆ ◆ ◆

BOOKS BY BILLY MAKIN

JIHAD 1 – The lost scriptures
JIHAD 2 – A bride for Allah
JIHAD 3 – In the name of the prophet
JIHAD 4 - THE FINAL SOLUTION
THE LIGER SYNDROME
O'MALLEY – The wrong package
THE SMILING PILL
REINCARNATION

<u>Teenage books</u>
THE AMAZING ADVENTURES
OF SPOTTY SPINDLE

<u>Comedy Books</u>
TITS and TEETH in Thailand
FISHING AND TESTICLES

Fishing Books
THE GOLDEN YEARS

◆ ◆ ◆

THE AUTHOR

An authentic and archetypal 1950's baby boomer.
Working class roots, with standards and values that evolved in the grim, dark satanic mills and coal mining towns of the North West of England

Grammar school and university educated.

Soldier, engineer, and entrepreneur.

Designer and creator of Europe's largest ever commercial fishery.

Left England for sunnier climes at the age of 50, whilst still retaining UK consultancy work.

Now living in Thailand, where together with his Thai wife, he runs two successful businesses in the entertainment industry.

Still writing for various UK publications.

Between bouts of fishing and beer appreciation, Billy Makin writes books, acquiring a rapidly expanding fan base and becoming recognized as one of the UK's most exciting novelists.

THE GOLDEN YEARS

"Is the earth really round?"

◆ ◆ ◆

Printed in Great Britain
by Amazon